No matter what darts the Devil throws at you
He can never win against the Word!

"If God waited on people to become perfect
before He anointed them
to preach, teach, lead or minister,
there would never be anyone worthy,
and the work would never get done.

God uses willing vessels, with weaknesses,
so His strength, power, and anointing,
can shine through,
and He can get the glory!"

Keith Hammond

Arsenal of Ammunition

Scriptural Support in Battle

Cover Layout and Interior Design: Keith Hammond

Lessons For Life Books

PUBLISHERS

LESSONSFORLIFEBOOKS.COM

LessonsForLifeBooks.com

⌷A Lessons For Life Book

Arsenal of Ammunition

*Scriptural Support
in Battle*

© 2016 by
Keith Hammond
is published by
Lessons for Life Books, Inc.
St. Paul, Minnesota 55116

ISBN-13: 978-1-938588-03-7
Printed in the U.S.A.
Unless otherwise indicated, all scripture, passages and verse quotations are from the Holy Bible, King James version.

Dedication

God Almighty,
I give you all the glory, honor, and praise
for all that you have done and still do in, to, and through, my life.
Thank you for Jesus the Christ and the Holy Spirit,
and for the redeeming power of your Love.

To my wife,
over 30 years together,
thank you for all your prayers and patience.

To my daughters,
my Love for you goes beyond words.
Many blessings to you both.

To my grand-kids,
it is a great joy
to be Blessed with your presence in our lives.

To the Hammond and Fitzpatrick families,
I pray that you will unite arm in arm one day
and allow yourselves to be encircled by
the healing power of God's Love.

W E A P O N S

Usable in battle.
Needed to defend yourself.
Helpful to withstand any attacks.
Required to destroy the darts of the Devil!

THE QUIVER
Built upon the base, the basis, the basics, and the benefits of our belief, the Quiver contains the foundation of why we do battle.

THE BULLETS
Meant to be loaded into a weapon and fired when needed.
Without ammunition you may easily be defeated.

THE BOMBS
Can be used up close or from a distance.
Do the most damage when combined with other weapons.

THE SHELLS
Shells carry contents that when used turn to shrapnel that spreads to and affects everything around it.

THE SWORDS
Have two sharp edges.
Cuts through the enemy going and coming.

THE DAGGERS
Useful for quick and immediate jabs and attacks.
Most effective when you're up close.

THE DRONES
When attacking from a distance you need to use wisdom
knowledge, understanding and prophecy.

THE MINES
Meant to be planted where they will damage enemy strongholds
when he least expects it.

THE MISSILES
Capable of destroying the enemy from anywhere at anytime.
Considered the strongest of all the weapons.

BATTLE BONUS
Four of my most favorite scriptures, verses and passages
and a challenge to you to write your own Study Summary!

**A Christian without scripture
is like a gun without bullets.**

Introduction

There will always be many things we haven't noticed or seen in the Bible, and mysteries God has yet to reveal to us, but most Christians know more about the Bible than they think they do. This book is a checklist. It is full of dozens of Bible facts listed page by page, with space to check off things you do know, and use a mark to remember to study those you don't.

Based on three scriptures that Jesus pulled from the book of Deuteronomy when He was tempted by the Devil in the desert after His consecration fast, this book gives every Christian a handbook to use for study, and help others do the same, in order to always have God's Word ready to fire back at the Devil when he throws darts at you. Why exactly does the devil throw darts at you? There are a few reasons but this is what I believe is the primary one:

The Devil has peeked into your future and is trying to stop you from walking into your calling and being wise enough to help win hundreds, or thousands or even millions of souls back to God through Christ.

It's simple really...if the Devil IS NOT causing trouble, havoc, and or creating chaos in your life, you ARE NOT a threat to him. And, now that you know the reason behind most of the 'I can't believe this is happening to me' stuff in your life it's time to back the Devil up off you.

Welcome To Your Arsenal

Keep this arsenal with you at all times because your life depends on it. If you are caught without it, or are unprepared to use it, you are spiritually weak and open to any attack the Devil throws at you. Satan has declared war against God and His children; that includes me, and it includes you.

This book is designed to provide you with weapons to use to help win the battle against every war the enemy wages in your life, in your church and in your ministry. Some of the battles that your arsenal will be used for include:

+ Keeping prayer in schools.

+ Keeping the man in his home and the head of his family.

+ Keeping the covenant and sanctity of marriage of one man one woman.

+ Keeping ourselves and our kids away from drugs and alcohol.

+ Keeping ourselves content with what God Blesses us with.

+ Keeping yourself and your family in church and active in the ministry.

+ Keeping yourself active in prayer, fasting, and study.

These things and more are how you build up your best defenses against the Devil and his army of demons. Without a defense you're already defeated.

The QUIVER

Built upon the base, the basis, the basics, and the benefits of our belief, the Quiver contains the foundation of why we do battle.

In the beginning God created the Heavens and the Earth.

Genesis 1:1

☐ **This Bible fact is something I know by heart.**

☐ **This Bible fact is something I need to study.**

SCRIPTURE NOTES

_____

_____

_____

_____

_____

_____

STUDY SUMMARY

This scripture is essential to have in your arsenal because the Devil is using the weak will of many Scientists to promote a lie, in the form of a theory and belief that a big bang occurred that caused the Earth and Heavens to form. Now, I don't know about you, but I have seen some explosions in my life both in person and on television, yet I have never seen a single one of them leave behind something that is as structured, sound, strong, serving, and sustaining as the Earth. The Earth and the Heavens are some of the most incredibly beautiful and wonderfully marvelous manifestations of God's glory and power that we could ever hope to see or imagine. Explosions cause destruction and what they leave behind does not, could not, and could never compare to the intelligent and unduplicable design that God Himself has created for us to enjoy while we're here on Earth waiting to live in eternity.

STUDY NOTES

_____

_____

_____

_____

_____

_____

_____

_____

_____

_____

God said, Let us make man in our own image after our likeness.

Genesis 1:26

☐ **This Bible fact is something I know by heart.**

☐ **This Bible fact is something I need to study.**

SCRIPTURE NOTES

_____

_____

_____

_____

_____

STUDY SUMMARY

This scripture is essential to have in your arsenal because until people come to terms with the fact that we are created to look like God and we are easily identifiable as being His children, mankind will never truly accept our role as children of the living God. We have been labeled as being descendants of everything from monkeys to aliens who were sent here to populate the planet. God is not mocked. He is the creator, ruler, and master of the universe. It is His. He did it without a laboratory, or science equipment, and theories. Man, however, needs all of these things just to study the DNA and other elements, which God created. Take away the DNA, or the egg that is solely responsible for merging with sperm to create another human, and science is left with absolutely nothing to study.

STUDY NOTES

_____

_____

_____

_____

_____

_____

_____

_____

_____

_____

God created man in His own image, in His own image created He him: male and female created He them.

Genesis 1:27

☐ **This Bible fact is something I know by heart.**

☐ **This Bible fact is something I need to study.**

SCRIPTURE NOTES

_____

_____

_____

_____

_____

_____

STUDY SUMMARY

This scripture is essential to have in your arsenal because the attack on marriage is so strong, that the very fabric of the covenant relationship between man and woman is being threatened. Those who choose to live life as homosexuals and sodomites make the decision to deny the will of God. While I have absolutely nothing against the individuals who make the lifestyle choices they make, the sins they commit in doing so I cannot condone or support. This is no different than thinking my own sins are OK and they are not. The type of sin does not matter from one to the next, sin is sin, and none of us have any business participating in it or promoting it. God is not mocked and His word has not changed. We will all stand before Him and give an account of our actions when our time comes.

STUDY NOTES

_____

_____

_____

_____

_____

_____

_____

_____

_____

_____

And God blessed the seventh day, and sancti-fied it: because that in it He had rested from all His work which God created and made.

Genesis 2:3

☐ This Bible fact is something I know by heart.

☐ This Bible fact is something I need to study.

SCRIPTURE NOTES

_____

_____

_____

_____

_____

_____

STUDY SUMMARY

This scripture is essential to have in your arsenal because many people do not understand the significance of the sabbath. From as far back as I can remember in my youth I've heard the term Seventh Day Adventist. I never really knew anything about them until I became a church leader, and began studying religion and relationship. Jesus said man was not made for the sabbath, but the sabbath for man. This is clear to me that we are not to worship the sabbath but to remember it. If you watch my video interview titled: *Tips For Taking Mission Trips* which you can see at PastorKeith.org you'll find that in the interview with two missionaries, they explain in detail how and why the sabbath is important and highly reverenced in places such as Israel. The Devil wants people to forget it altogether so use this scripture to remind him of the reasons God blessed the sabbath and also sanctified it.

STUDY NOTES

_____

_____

_____

_____

_____

_____

_____

_____

_____

_____

And the name of the second river is Gihon: the same is it that compasseth the whole land of Ethiopia.

Genesis 2:13b

☐ **This Bible fact is something I know by heart.**

☐ **This Bible fact is something I need to study.**

SCRIPTURE NOTES

_____

_____

_____

_____

_____

STUDY SUMMARY

This scripture is essential to have in your arsenal because many people are unaware and do not believe that Biblical creation began in Africa. The fact that all the animals are still there, and that when Adam and Eve were evicted from the Garden of Eden, those who came after them eventually migrated north and came to settle in and around Jerusalem. Many who are in support of a 'white only' history, or of 'wiping out any race except white' or of 'ignoring the contribution of blacks in society altogether' may not listen to what the Bible has to say about the subject, but early in the book of Genesis, this passage of scripture exists. Use it when you are in battle against such narrow minded opposition as the truth is the only things that sets us free.

STUDY NOTES

_____

_____

_____

_____

_____

_____

_____

_____

_____

_____

_____

END OF CHAPTER
READING SUGGESTION

+ Genesis 1:1 to Genesis 2:25

The
BULLETS

Meant to be loaded into a weapon and fired when needed.
Without ammunition you may easily be defeated.

And the Lord God took the man and put him into the Garden of Eden to dress it and keep it.

Genesis 2:15

☐ **This Bible fact is something I know by heart.**

☐ **This Bible fact is something I need to study.**

SCRIPTURE NOTES

_____

_____

_____

_____

_____

_____

STUDY SUMMARY

This scripture is essential to have in your arsenal because man's place was in paradise. God created it, established it, placed food and sustenance in it, gave us companionship, and built a hedge of protection around it. All we had to do was maintain it. This scripture is helpful when you have to teach or expand on lessons about creation, Adam and Eve, the Garden of Eden, or anything related to how and what happened that made God choose to evict them from the Garden and curse them, rather than forgive them and give second chances. Further in Genesis, in the times of Noah, you'll find that God made the decision to destroy mankind, unleashed a flood, which killed everything except Noah, his family, selected animals, and the reason behind the fall of man in the Garden due to sin, which is Satan.

STUDY NOTES

_____

_____

_____

_____

_____

_____

_____

_____

_____

_____

And the Lord God commanded the man, saying, Of every tree of the garden thou mayest freely eat:

Genesis 2:16

☐ **This Bible fact is something I know by heart.**

☐ **This Bible fact is something I need to study.**

SCRIPTURE NOTES

_____

_____

_____

_____

_____

_____

STUDY SUMMARY

This scripture is essential to have in your arsenal because when God created all the plants, animals, and told Adam what was good to eat and what wasn't, that should have been the end of it. Yet, during a moment when Eve was alone she was approached and tricked by the Devil into believing that God did not *really* mean that she and Adam would die if they ate of the tree of the knowledge of good and evil. Satan went so far as to convince her that God was only concerned with her and Adam becoming like gods, knowing good and evil. Instead of Eve calling on or consulting Adam on the subject, and informing him of her conversation with the culprit, she decided that she was going to eat of the tree, and then feed some of the fruit to Adam as well. Use this scripture anytime you need to remember or remind others that what God says...goes...period. When God gives you a command simply comply.

STUDY NOTES

_____

_____

_____

_____

_____

_____

_____

_____

_____

But of the tree of the knowledge of good and evil, thou shalt not eat of it: for in the day that thou eatest thereof thou shalt surely die. **Genesis 2:17**

☐ **This Bible fact is something I know by heart.**

☐ **This Bible fact is something I need to study.**

SCRIPTURE NOTES

_____

_____

_____

_____

_____

_____

STUDY SUMMARY

This scripture is essential to have in your arsenal because if we cannot comply with a simply command, then God cannot and should not trust us. When we are teaching or preaching or reaching out to others with lessons that center around obedience to God's command, this scripture is hugely helpful in that it is the base of who we were as children of God, long before we ever became committed to Christ. Our very essence existed before Jesus died on the cross for our sins, and before we ever came to know Him as our Lord and Savior. This scripture is also useful as a weapon of war against the enemy who obviously didn't heed God's word and took it upon himself to try and overthrow God. Before Satan was able to convince Eve to eat and subsequently feed a sin-laced apple to Adam, Satan was able to convince a third of the Angels who were already in Heaven to follow his advice too. As a result, all of them were evicted from Heaven, and are destined for Hell.

STUDY NOTES

_____

_____

_____

_____

_____

_____

_____

_____

_____

_____

And the rib, which the Lord God had taken from man, made He a woman, and brought her unto the man.

Genesis 2:22

☐ **This Bible fact is something I know by heart.**

☐ **This Bible fact is something I need to study.**

SCRIPTURE NOTES

_____

_____

_____

_____

_____

_____

STUDY SUMMARY

This scripture is essential to have in your arsenal because man was never meant to do anything alone. We need others, especially when we are married, to walk with us, side-by-side, to accomplish many of the tasks we either set out to do, or are given by God to do. One of the first things God created after the Heavens and the Earth was man, so we could become part of His family. And even though there were countless animals on land and in the seas, God Himself says in Genesis 2:18 that it is not good for man to be alone. Thus, God created woman out of man, thereby making a first family. This scripture is useful against attacks that bring into question the Biblical standard of relationships between man and woman, and why is it vital to keep God's context in such relationships intact.

STUDY NOTES

_____

_____

_____

_____

_____

_____

_____

_____

_____

_____

Therefore shall a man leave his father and his mother, and shall cleave unto his wife: and they shall be one flesh.

Genesis 2:24

☐ **This Bible fact is something I know by heart.**

☐ **This Bible fact is something I need to study.**

SCRIPTURE NOTES

_____

_____

_____

_____

_____

_____

STUDY SUMMARY

This scripture is essential to have in your arsenal because in this modern society, the attack against marriage is so strong that people are slowly giving into the notion that two women are OK to be married; and two men are OK to be married. This is totally and completely against God, against His law, and against His will. There is also a long standing attack against marriage from within families in that drama can come from mother-in-laws trying to hold on to their sons; dads trying to hold on to their adult daughters; and if we simply learn to trust God and stay out of other people's marriages even if they are within our family, or even if they are our kids, we would be much better off.

STUDY NOTES

_____

_____

_____

_____

_____

_____

_____

_____

_____

_____

_____

And the eyes of them both were opened, and they knew that they were naked; and they sewed fig leaves together, and made themselves aprons.

Genesis 3:7

☐ **This Bible fact is something I know by heart.**

☐ **This Bible fact is something I need to study.**

SCRIPTURE NOTES

_____

_____

_____

_____

_____

_____

STUDY SUMMARY

This scripture is essential to have in your arsenal because once Adam and Eve became aware that they were human beings, their life as spiritual beings began to end. And before Christ came to sacrifice His life and offer us the free gift of salvation in place of eternal damnation, there was no coming back from spiritual death. Adam and Eve were evicted from the Garden of Eden, cursed for their disobedience, and made to suffer punishment that has endured for centuries, such as pain in childbirth. God eventually made clothes for Adam and Eve from animals skins rather than the leaves they used, which covered their physical bodies but did nothing for the state of their spiritual relationship with Him. This scripture is helpful when teaching what it means to be spiritually naked without a Godly covering.

STUDY NOTES

_____

_____

_____

_____

_____

_____

_____

_____

_____

_____

And He said, who told thee that thou wast naked? Hast thou eaten of the tree, whereof I commanded thee that thou shouldest not eat?

Genesis 3:11

☐ **This Bible fact is something I know by heart.**

☐ **This Bible fact is something I need to study.**

SCRIPTURE NOTES

_____

_____

_____

_____

_____

_____

STUDY SUMMARY

This scripture is essential to have in your arsenal because Adam and Eve were never meant to know about certain things. Their eyes were never meant to see certain things. This scripture is helpful for us to remember that when God commands us to do something, that the only way the Devil can ever intervene between what God tells us to do, and what we follow through and do, is if we are disobedient to God and listen to either the Devil or our own thoughts, or follow after what our eyes can see. The Bible says that Eve was likely mesmerized by what she saw, the beauty of the tree, and her limited thinking that it would make one wise, that she did eat of the fruit, and gave some to Adam, and he did eat. The Bible places emphasis on the fact that her eyes played a big part in what took place, which is why we as Christians today, must be mindful of what we allow our eyes to see, because they truly are the windows to our soul.

STUDY NOTES

_____

_____

_____

_____

_____

_____

_____

_____

_____

And the Lord God said unto the serpent, Because thou hast done this, thou art cursed above all cattle, and above every beast of the field; upon thy belly shalt thou go, and dust shalt thou eat all the days of thy life. **Genesis 3:14**

☐ This Bible fact is something I know by heart.

☐ This Bible fact is something I need to study.

SCRIPTURE NOTES

_____

_____

_____

_____

_____

_____

STUDY SUMMARY

This scripture is essential to have in your arsenal because this curse is what the Devil knows added to his punishment of being evicted from Heaven. The more we remind Satan of it, the worst off he will be. The more you bring it back to his remembrance, the less he will want to try and bother you. In addition, once we learn the result of disobedience we are not likely to do what someone else did. When you see someone lose their life, you may want to keep yours; or when you see someone else fall into a ditch, you may want to walk around it; or when you notice someone committing a crime, you may want to walk the other way. This scripture is very helpful when teaching one of the things that can happen when we disobey God.

STUDY NOTES

_____

_____

_____

_____

_____

_____

_____

_____

_____

_____

_____

And the Lord God said, Behold, the man is become as one of us, to know good and evil: and now, lest he put forth his hand, and take also of the tree of life, and eat, and live for ever:

Genesis 3:22

☐ **This Bible fact is something I know by heart.**

☐ **This Bible fact is something I need to study.**

SCRIPTURE NOTES

_____

_____

_____

_____

_____

_____

STUDY SUMMARY

This scripture is essential to have in your arsenal because mankind was created by God to be spiritual beings living in fleshly bodies. We were never meant to know anything about our flesh, until God wanted us to; we were never meant to have any interaction with evil, and although Adam was guilty by association, he received a similar sentence as the other two. God had given us everything that He made, which is good, but Satan, who had already been exiled to Earth, seemed bent on revenge, and saw his opportunity to try and destroy what God had created and the relationship between God and man. Our relationship with God has never been the same and until Satan is destroyed for good, and sin is no longer a force in people's lives, it never will be.

STUDY NOTES

_____

_____

_____

_____

_____

_____

_____

_____

_____

_____

END OF CHAPTER
READING SUGGESTION

+ Genesis 2:1 to Genesis 3:24

The BOMBS

Can be used up close or from a distance.
Do the most damage when combined with other weapons.

If thou doest well, shalt thou not be accepted? And if thou doest not well, sin lieth at the door. And unto thee shall be his desire, and thou shalt rule over him.

Genesis 4:7

☐ This Bible fact is something I know by heart.

☐ This Bible fact is something I need to study.

SCRIPTURE NOTES

_____

_____

_____

_____

_____

_____

STUDY SUMMARY

This scripture is essential to have in your arsenal because there are many times in our lives where the Devil will try and tempt us with things. It is at those times that this scripture needs to be remembered so that what God told Cain becomes relevant to us. The same rule applies in that if we do well and praise God for it by giving him the firstfruit of our increase, then all will be well with us. However, if and when we don't, then the same curse that was counted to Cain, will also affect us. For example, this scripture can be very helpful in classroom situations using the scenario where you have two students assigned to one project. One student gives their all and the teacher is well pleased; but the other student puts in little effort, but wants the same credit and accolades as the other student. God says do well, and all will be well with you. Anything less, and Satan will be waiting to claim you as his.

STUDY NOTES

And now are thou cursed from the Earth, which hath opened her mouth to receive thy brother's blood from thy hand:

Genesis 4:11

☐ **This Bible fact is something I know by heart.**

☐ **This Bible fact is something I need to study.**

SCRIPTURE NOTES

_____

_____

_____

_____

_____

_____

STUDY SUMMARY

This scripture is essential to have in your arsenal because the settling of sin on the men and women who were trying to learn how to live life God's way was interrupted once sin entered in. Cain killing Abel caused God to curse both the man, his method, any place he should live and anyone who tried to end his life along the way. God even marked Cain to keep others from killing him. Cain thought the punishment did not fit the crime, although we know that God is very serious about the shedding of man's blood, especially when it is not in the context of war, and when it is innocent. This scripture is helpful when teaching lessons such as *Am I My Brother's Keeper* and for showing siblings how and why to respect one another because God is always and will always be watching.

STUDY NOTES

_____

_____

_____

_____

_____

_____

_____

_____

_____

_____

Whoso sheddeth man's blood, by man shall his blood be shed: for in the image of God made he man.

Genesis 9:6

☐ This Bible fact is something I know by heart.

☐ This Bible fact is something I need to study.

SCRIPTURE NOTES

_____

_____

_____

_____

_____

_____

STUDY SUMMARY

This scripture is essential to have in your arsenal because the Devil already knows his fate, and the book of Revelation chapter 20 verse 10 is clear on that. In today's society, even though we are just a few short decades beyond the civil rights movement, black on black crime is at an all time high. While white people's atrocities against blacks played a huge part in it, it will take love for your fellow man to overcome this problem. Black people of all ages need to be told and be reminded that if anything prompts them to shed man's blood, that man shall also be the one to shed his. This seems not to scare young black men who believe the gun is their god, possibly because they've never heard God's word in this context read into their ears. Faith comes by hearing and hearing by the word of God, and one cannot hear without a preacher. Thus, if they've never heard a sermon or immersed themselves in faith, church and ministry, this notion is likely foreign to them.

STUDY NOTES

_____

_____

_____

_____

_____

_____

_____

_____

And I will bless them that bless thee, and curse him that curseth thee: and in thee shall all families of the Earth be blessed.

Genesis 12:3

☐ **This Bible fact is something I know by heart.**

☐ **This Bible fact is something I need to study.**

SCRIPTURE NOTES

_____

_____

_____

_____

_____

STUDY SUMMARY

This scripture is essential to have in your arsenal because God makes a covenant with Abram as the leader of many nations. As parents we have to be the ones to do battle for our children until they are ready and mature enough to defend themselves both physically and spiritually. We have to be the ones to walk the floor at night in prayer while they are sleeping so they have an advocate to help them both in their dreams, and in the daytime. We are responsible for their state of mind and the matters of their heart until they are old enough to learn the lessons we have been taught through Bible study and from God's presence in our lives by way of the work of the Holy Spirit. As parents, this scripture speaks volumes as to how eye for an eye works in God's eyes, and when teaching our children that they have an advocate in Heaven who is greater, stronger and much more powerful than their parents.

STUDY NOTES

_____

_____

_____

_____

_____

_____

_____

_____

_____

_____

I am the God of thy father, the God of Abraham, the God of Isaac, and the God of Jacob.

Exodus 3:6

☐ **This Bible fact is something I know by heart.**

☐ **This Bible fact is something I need to study.**

SCRIPTURE NOTES

_____

_____

_____

_____

_____

_____

STUDY SUMMARY

This scripture is essential to have in your arsenal because God identifies Himself to Moses. This is important because Moses had been wandering in the wilderness after being exiled from the only life he knew, and driven into a land he has never known. Remember, Moses was a Hebrew baby, placed in a basket to save his life from the death decree. He was rescued from the water by an Egyptian woman and raised in the palace with Pharoah. This scripture is stupendous for teaching students lessons that show that God in fact does have compassion for people; that He can use anyone no matter what they have done; that we can be raised one way, with no connection to the ministry, and when Jesus comes into our life, we can become what it is that we have been called and purposed to be. The Devil has been trying to overthrow God since he was in Heaven, and this is one way to remind him of who is really in control, and always will be.

STUDY NOTES

_____

_____

_____

_____

_____

_____

_____

_____

_____

The Lord shall fight for you and you shall hold your peace.

Exodus 14:14

☐ **This Bible fact is something I know by heart.**

☐ **This Bible fact is something I need to study.**

SCRIPTURE NOTES

_____

_____

_____

_____

_____

_____

STUDY SUMMARY

This scripture is essential to have in your arsenal because when attacks come against us there is one thing that we can always take into battle. It is our construct, our confidence, and our comfort. One song says *The Battle is Not Yours* another says *Jesus Will Fix It* and many others elude to the fact that it does not matter how many battles the enemy brings, or how many issues he initiates, we can stand still and see the salvation of The Lord. When God fights our battles for us, He always win. But when we fight alone, we never do. Without God we can do nothing. He is our fortress, our shield and buckler, our battleaxe, and all the things we could ever hope to take into battle. This scripture is great for teaching young people being bullied that if they hold their peace, God will eventually step in and holding them up, even if that means tearing others down in order to get His message across that mistreating people is not OK, especially when they can't defend themselves.

STUDY NOTES

_____

_____

_____

_____

_____

_____

_____

_____

_____

Thy right hand O Lord, is become glorious in power: thy right hand, O Lord, hath dashed in pieces the enemy.

Exodus 15:6

☐ **This Bible fact is something I know by heart.**

☐ **This Bible fact is something I need to study.**

SCRIPTURE NOTES

_____

_____

_____

_____

_____

_____

STUDY SUMMARY

This scripture is essential to have in your arsenal because the Devil cannot stand up against God. Because we are children of the Most High God, we are afforded the protections that come along with being heirs to His throne and His Kingdom. When we give our wants and our will over to God, it is He that blesses us with the things we want, the victories over the enemy, the brilliance to defeat all our enemies in battle. God's power is power. When He fights the battle on our behalf, we always win. It is only when we try to attempt and do things on our own; go our own way; hear God but do not listen to Him; see God's way but do not follow it; then we are left to our own devices, defenseless against the work of the Devil. This scripture can help teach lessons about it making sense to follow someone greater than us.

STUDY NOTES

_____

_____

_____

_____

_____

_____

_____

_____

_____

_____

The enemy said, I will pursue, I will overtake, I will divide the spoil; my lust shall be satisfied upon them; I will draw my sword, my hand shall destroy them.

Exodus 15:9

☐ **This Bible fact is something I know by heart.**

☐ **This Bible fact is something I need to study.**

SCRIPTURE NOTES

_____

_____

_____

_____

_____

_____

STUDY SUMMARY

This scripture is essential to have in your arsenal because the Devil is so stuck on himself, that everything he speaks of is about himself. Satan still believes he has power to overthrow God even after he was evicted from Heaven, sent to Earth, and banished to Hell for all eternity. He says, I, I, I, instead of 'thy', 'thy', thy'. As children of God, we should know, recognize and understand that always thinking about just ourselves is selfish and sinful. As cliche` as it sounds *there is no 'i' in team or in 'us' or in 'God' or in 'Jesus' or in 'we'* and these are the words and the ways that the Devil wants us not to focus on but rather follow after his foolishness, which will have us nowhere and doing nothing but waiting to spend eternity in Hell with him.

STUDY NOTES

_____

_____

_____

_____

_____

_____

_____

_____

_____

_____

_____

_____

I am the Lord thy God which have brought thee out of the land of Egypt, out of the house of bondage.

Exodus 20:2

☐ **This Bible fact is something I know by heart.**

☐ **This Bible fact is something I need to study.**

SCRIPTURE NOTES

_____

_____

_____

_____

_____

_____

STUDY SUMMARY

This scripture is essential to have in your arsenal because God wants us to know and to understand that when we pray to Him He will answer us. The problem we have is that we want God to move in our time, in our way, and for our purpose. This scriptures is the standard and sets the stage for the onset and the introduction of the Ten Commandments. God wants us to always remember that it was Him who delivered His people out of bondage. He is the one who heard their cries and answered their prayer. He is the one who moved in their situation of slavery and because they trusted in Him, He worked against Pharoah on their behalf. The scripture is helpful in today's context because many of us have been through situations of slavery in one way or another, and we can use it to remind us to look to God for freedom.

STUDY NOTES

_____

_____

_____

_____

_____

_____

_____

_____

_____

END OF CHAPTER
READING SUGGESTION

+ Genesis 4:1 to Exodus 19:25

The SHELLS

Shells carry contents that when used turn to shrapnel that spreads to and affects everything around it.

Thou shalt have no other gods before me.

Exodus 20:3

☐ **This Bible fact is something I know by heart.**

☐ **This Bible fact is something I need to study.**

SCRIPTURE NOTES

_____

_____

_____

_____

_____

_____

STUDY SUMMARY

This scripture is essential to have in your arsenal because it is the first of Ten Commandments that God gave to man so that we would know the rules He expects us to live by. These are the standards and the structure that we are to follow to live our lives patterned after. This scripture is helpful alone or when using it with the other nine to teach lessons of why we should love God and worship Him, and follow after Jesus the Christ who not only died in our place, but ushered in grace and salvation so that we would be able to live and experience life at a much higher level than those on the planet who make the conscious decision to deny God.

STUDY NOTES

_____

_____

_____

_____

_____

_____

_____

_____

_____

_____

_____

_____

Thou shalt not make unto thee any graven image.

Exodus 20:4

☐ **This Bible fact is something I know by heart.**

☐ **This Bible fact is something I need to study.**

SCRIPTURE NOTES

_____

_____

_____

_____

_____

_____

STUDY SUMMARY

This scripture is essential to have in your arsenal because it is the part of the Ten Commandments that God wants us to understand is one of the things that can mess us up the most. The Lord spends a lot of time in scripture taking about the dangers of serving other gods or following after idols. The demonic spirits and influences that come along with such activity can take control of our flesh and have us doing and participating in some of the most ungodly activity that we can imagine. This scripture is imperative for lessons that teach for example the message of how Satan can use simple words such as '*idol*' on a TV show about singing to draw you into the worship of people instead of the one who created the people. Remember, the way that the Devil tricked Eve was simply by twisting the words in God's command that she and Adam would die if they ate from the tree of the knowledge of good and evil. They could have avoided spiritual death by simply being obedient.

STUDY NOTES

_____

_____

_____

_____

_____

_____

_____

_____

_____

Thou shalt not take the name of the Lord thy God in vain.

Exodus 20:7

☐ This Bible fact is something I know by heart.

☐ This Bible fact is something I need to study.

SCRIPTURE NOTES

_____

_____

_____

_____

_____

STUDY SUMMARY

This scripture is essential to have in your arsenal because God's name is sacred and Holy and hallowed and it is to be revered and respected and not used in any context or content that does not honor Him for who He is. Taking God's name in vane is one of the most egregious sins on the planet but people in the world do it often. Christians are somewhat more mindful of being careful not to let themselves stoop to this level, but the ungodly and worldly influences on television, radio, and the Internet, are so prevalent and so pervasive and persuasive that even the most anointed of Christians have to stay prayed up and full of fasting to keep themselves from this sin. Once you have given yourself over to using God's name as if it's just any other name, it is very difficult to come back from this practice. The generations of young people coming up behind us are the ones who need to be taught this the most because they are facing temptations that we never experienced.

STUDY NOTES

_____

_____

_____

_____

_____

_____

_____

_____

_____

Remember the sabbath day to keep it holy.

Exodus 20:8

☐ **This Bible fact is something I know by heart.**

☐ **This Bible fact is something I need to study.**

SCRIPTURE NOTES

_____

_____

_____

_____

_____

_____

STUDY SUMMARY

This scripture is essential to have in your arsenal because in the beginning of the Holy Bible, God laid out days, weeks, months, and years for us to use as a guideline for calendars. But long before He gave us days, He blessed the sabbath and sanctified it. Man has long since begun to take it upon himself to worship on any day of the week, and while worship whenever it happens is an incredible thing, God still does things decent and in order. He wants us to remember the sabbath to keep it holy, meaning that instead of putting on programs to honor pastors, and anniversaries, and special days and events, God wants us to honor and recognize the sabbath for what He created it to be, so it remains a part of our worship, and our way of remembering ourselves and reminding others of who He is. Six days of labor and work, but the seventh day is the sabbath where we abstain from work and all labor.

STUDY NOTES

_____

_____

_____

_____

_____

_____

_____

_____

_____

_____

Honor thy father and thy mother.

Exodus 20:12

☐ **This Bible fact is something I know by heart.**

☐ **This Bible fact is something I need to study.**

SCRIPTURE NOTES

_____

_____

_____

_____

_____

_____

STUDY SUMMARY

This scripture is essential to have in your arsenal because it is the reminder from God Himself that our Earthly parents are to be honored and respected. Many young people in today's society have gotten ahead of themselves and think they don't need their parents telling them what to do, and they look to the Internet and social media and their circle of friends and every other ungodly influence on the planet to make them believe that their parents are just the people who pay their bills and give them rules to follow. God wants us to honor and respect our parents so much that He made it one of the Ten Commandments. There are millions of other scriptures in the Bible, but this was given as one of the most important. How we all treat this scripture may indeed teach us life lessons that we could otherwise never learn, especially when parents who took care of us get older and need us to care for them.

STUDY NOTES

_____

_____

_____

_____

_____

_____

_____

_____

_____

Thou shalt not kill.

Exodus 20:13

☐ **This Bible fact is something I know by heart.**

☐ **This Bible fact is something I need to study.**

SCRIPTURE NOTES

_____

_____

_____

_____

_____

_____

STUDY SUMMARY

This scripture is essential to have in your arsenal because it is one of the Devil's methods for keeping God's people from pursuing all that God would have us to become, and prospering in every area of our life that God orders our steps into. Jesus taught that the Devil comes to steal, kill, and destroy. This in itself should be enough for each of us to turn to God for answers and for Him to intervene on our behalf in these last days and perilous times. There are children dying in the streets, there are some in authority doing the killing, there are kids killing other kids, there are people killing the dreams of others by stepping over them and pushing them back because of greed and power. There are many forms of killing, and God wants us to remember and be mindful that He wants each of us to reach our full potential in life, in the church and in the ministry.

STUDY NOTES

_____

_____

_____

_____

_____

_____

_____

_____

_____

_____

Thou shalt not commit adultery.

Exodus 20:14

☐ **This Bible fact is something I know by heart.**

☐ **This Bible fact is something I need to study.**

SCRIPTURE NOTES

_____

_____

_____

_____

_____

_____

STUDY SUMMARY

This scripture is essential to have in your arsenal because have you ever thought about the different types of adultery? There are commonly two types: (1) Physical and (2) Spiritual. Although physical adultery is the one most often talked about and the one most referenced on the planet when we talk about or think about how most marriages end. However, the Devil himself and all the Angels that he convinced to follow him, all committed spiritual adultery in Heaven against God long before they ever came to Earth, man was created, and humans ever became familiar with the term. The Devil wants us to forget about spiritual adultery and focus on physical adultery so that we never think about how dangerous and destructive and detrimental spiritual adultery is to our life and to our ministry.

STUDY NOTES

_____

_____

_____

_____

_____

_____

_____

_____

_____

_____

_____

Thou shalt not steal.

Exodus 20:15

☐ **This Bible fact is something I know by heart.**

☐ **This Bible fact is something I need to study.**

SCRIPTURE NOTES

_____

_____

_____

_____

_____

STUDY SUMMARY

This scripture is essential to have in your arsenal because taking something that doesn't belong to you is another one of the ways the Devil showed his wickedness and caused him to be evicted from Heaven. In today's society people seem to have no boundaries about taking things that do not belong to them. We see evidence of it in all facets of society but the most glaring cases and examples are in corporate greed, banking, law, politics, and many other high level areas. But on the bottom tiers of our value system, theft is very prevalent as well. Greed is the most common factor, and this scripture should be coupled with the one in the book of Timothy, which says that having food and clothing we should be content. Being content with what we have is the formula for how we get more. God's word says that if we are faithful over a few things, that He will trust us with more. It took me a long time to learn this lesson personally, but I thank God I finally did.

STUDY NOTES

_____

_____

_____

_____

_____

_____

_____

_____

Thou shalt not bear false witness against thy neighbor.

Exodus 20:16

☐ **This Bible fact is something I know by heart.**

☐ **This Bible fact is something I need to study.**

SCRIPTURE NOTES

_____

_____

_____

_____

_____

STUDY SUMMARY

This scripture is essential to have in your arsenal because Jesus showed us that lying is the Devil's language. No Christian should ever be participating in it. The world is full of it within many of the people and especially many professions such as politics and lawyers and policing. Christians have to set the standard and allow the Holy Spirit to guide us into all truth. In my video lesson, which is #110 at PastorKeith.org/videos I teach that in order for us to communicate with God we must speak His language. God does not lie. If we ever expect to hold a conversation with Him or anticipate Him listening to our prayers, they must be completely truthful. This is a great lesson to teach children who seem to pick up lying out of the air, or from their parents. Teaching them that no matter what happens or who may be hurt by it, the truth is what the Bible says always sets us free.

STUDY NOTES

_____

_____

_____

_____

_____

_____

_____

_____

_____

_____

Thou shalt not covet.

Exodus 20:17

☐ **This Bible fact is something I know by heart.**

☐ **This Bible fact is something I need to study.**

SCRIPTURE NOTES

_____

_____

_____

_____

_____

_____

STUDY SUMMARY

This scripture is essential to have in your arsenal because our society is full of people who spend most of their time trying to keep up with the *Joneses*. Television is chock full of reality shows that promote the concept that your life isn't worth much unless you have what certain people have; earn what they earn; buy what they buy; and so on. This *false reality* is beyond the realm of what is and should be *the norm* for living a Christian lifestyle. In Matthew 6:31 to 33 Jesus teaches that if we concentrate on seeking first the Kingdom of God, that all these *things* shall be added unto us. Although we cannot have what does not belong to us or what God has not given unto us. Coveting our neighbor's wives or husbands goes against everything that the Bible teaches. When anyone we know receives a blessing in the form of a new job, promotion, house, car, or anything of material value, we should simply be happy for them rather than spending any time praying to receive it.

STUDY NOTES

_____

_____

_____

_____

_____

_____

_____

_____

END OF CHAPTER
READING SUGGESTION

+ Genesis 20:1 to Genesis 24:18

The SWORDS

Have two sharp edges.
Cuts through the enemy going and coming.

If ye walk in my statutes, and keep my commandments, and do them; Then I will give you rain in due season, and the land shall yield her increase, and the trees of the field shall yield their fruit.

Leviticus 26:3-4

☐ **This Bible fact is something I know by heart.**

☐ **This Bible fact is something I need to study.**

SCRIPTURE NOTES

_____

_____

_____

_____

_____

_____

STUDY SUMMARY

This scripture is essential to have in your arsenal because God's statutes, His commandments, rain, and fruit, are all types of blessings. Typically when we think of blessings, we may list a new house, new car, new job, new spouse, promotion, more money, and so on, but the way God blesses us, long before these *things* ever enter the picture, is with the *standards* of His riches in Heaven. The wealth of Heaven is an abundance of life, good health, favor, protection, leadership in His church and ministries, and one scripture says He will even make your enemies be at peace with you. The fruit of the Lord is the real benefit and you are certainly blessed if you are receiving it.

STUDY NOTES

_____

_____

_____

_____

_____

_____

_____

_____

_____

_____

_____

Thou shalt fear the Lord thy God, and serve Him, and shalt swear by His name.

Deuteronomy 6:13

☐ **This Bible fact is something I know by heart.**

☐ **This Bible fact is something I need to study.**

SCRIPTURE NOTES

_____

_____

_____

_____

_____

_____

STUDY SUMMARY

This scripture is essential to have in your arsenal because this is one of the scriptures that Jesus used against the Devil when being tempted during His Fast in the wilderness. After Jesus was baptized by John the Baptist the Holy Spirit descended upon Him like a dove and God's voice was heard acknowledging Jesus as His son by saying He was well pleased. Because Jesus used this scripture to fend of an attack from Satan, so should you. It is a simple scripture to remember, and to recall when needed, and I highly recommend you make it part of your arsenal of ammunition, and keep it as one of those at the very top of your list and your life.

STUDY NOTES

_____

_____

_____

_____

_____

_____

_____

_____

_____

_____

_____

Ye shall not tempt the Lord your God, as ye tempted Him in Massah.

Deuteronomy 6:16

☐ **This Bible fact is something I know by heart.**

☐ **This Bible fact is something I need to study.**

SCRIPTURE NOTES

_____

_____

_____

_____

_____

_____

STUDY SUMMARY

This scripture is essential to have in your arsenal because as another of the three scriptures that Jesus used against an attack by the Devil while Fasting 40 days and 40 nights, this scripture is a sword against Satan. Jesus referred to a previous event, most likely in Heaven, before Satan was banished to Earth, and exiled to spend eternity in Hell. This event was recalled by Jesus when Satan prompted Him to do something to help Himself so He wouldn't suffer as much through the Fast. Suffering during any sacrifice is the point. The Fast is the focus. Jesus stayed the course, did not waver, and sent the Devil on His way, using this scripture as the sword that struck Satan right where it was needed.

STUDY NOTES

_____

_____

_____

_____

_____

_____

_____

_____

_____

_____

_____

Man doth not live by bread only, but by every word that proceedeth out of the mouth of the Lord doth man live.

Deuteronomy 8:3

☐ **This Bible fact is something I know by heart.**

☐ **This Bible fact is something I need to study.**

SCRIPTURE NOTES

_____

_____

_____

_____

_____

STUDY SUMMARY

This scripture is essential to have in your arsenal because as the last of three scriptures Jesus used against Satan while being tempted during His Fast, this verse let the Devil know that Jesus need earthly food to sustain Himself. The word of God is sufficient for the day. This scripture is a powerful and truly dynamic way to remind yourself that earthly food, even though the nutrition that is created by God sustains our bodies, the food that comes from eating of God's word is much more vital and infinitely more important to us in the Spirit. Teaching people to use this scripture while they are Fasting is another way to use it as a sword against the Devil.

STUDY NOTES

_____

_____

_____

_____

_____

_____

_____

_____

_____

_____

_____

_____

For the Lord thy God walketh in the midst of thy camp, to deliver thee, and to give up thine enemies before thee; therefore shall thy camp be holy: that he see no unclean thing in thee, and turn away from thee.

Deuteronomy 24:13

☐ **This Bible fact is something I know by heart.**

☐ **This Bible fact is something I need to study.**

SCRIPTURE NOTES

_____

_____

_____

_____

_____

_____

STUDY SUMMARY

This scripture is essential to have in your arsenal because when we seek God's help in battle against our enemies, the Lord wants us to be upright and doing what is right before we seek His input. He does not want to come down, inspect our Spiritual house, and find anything unclean within us. If He does, the Bible says He will turn away from us. This is the very reason why it is imperative that we live out lives in His will and His way, so that we may walk circumspectly in the world, without spot or wrinkle, so that when we need God's help for something, His inspection of the problem and of the person with the problem will prompt Him to intervene rather than turn away.

STUDY NOTES

_____

_____

_____

_____

_____

_____

_____

_____

_____

_____

_____

_____

There shall not any man be able to stand before thee all the days of thy life: as I was with Moses, so I will be with thee: I will not fail thee, nor forsake thee.

Joshua 1:5

☐ **This Bible fact is something I know by heart.**

☐ **This Bible fact is something I need to study.**

SCRIPTURE NOTES

_____

_____

_____

_____

_____

_____

STUDY SUMMARY

This scripture is essential to have in your arsenal because after Moses had been used by God to deliver the people of Israel from the bondage of slavery in Egypt, God chose Joshua as the next leader when it was time for Moses to die. God's conversation with Joshua is not unlike His instruction to us when we are stepping up to positions of leadership in the church and in the ministry. He wants us to trust Him. He wants us to rely on Him. He wants us to stand with Him. And if we do these things, He promises to never leave us nor forsake us nor fail us. This scripture is helpful for giving you hope when you need help.

STUDY NOTES

_____

_____

_____

_____

_____

_____

_____

_____

_____

_____

_____

And if it seem evil unto you to serve the Lord, choose you this day whom ye will serve; whether the gods which your fathers served that were on the other side of the flood, or the gods of the Amorites, in whose land ye dwell: but as for me and my house, we will serve the Lord.

Joshua 24:15

☐ **This Bible fact is something I know by heart.**

☐ **This Bible fact is something I need to study.**

SCRIPTURE NOTES

_____

_____

_____

_____

_____

_____

STUDY SUMMARY

This scripture is essential to have in your arsenal because as the new leader of the people of Israel, Joshua made it a point to stand up before the people and remind them that they have to make a choice to either serve God or prepare to perish as Pharoah did. This scripture is an incredible tool to use when teaching how God shows us that He can make our enemies our footstool when we are in His favor. God's favor comes with certain protections that keep us victorious in battle. His favor not only comes with the weapons we need to fight the battle, but the strategy for what to do while we are going through.

STUDY NOTES

_____

_____

_____

_____

_____

_____

_____

_____

_____

_____

_____

And David spake unto the Lord the words of this song in the day that the Lord had delivered him out of the hand of all his enemies, and out of the hand of Saul: And he said, The Lord is my rock, and my fortress, and my deliverer; The God of my rock; in Him will I trust: He is my shield, and the horn of my salvation, my high tower, and my refuge, my saviour; thou savest me from violence. I will call on the Lord, who is worthy to be praised: so shall I be saved from mine enemies.

2nd Samuel 22:1-4

☐ **This Bible fact is something I know by heart.**

☐ **This Bible fact is something I need to study.**

SCRIPTURE NOTES

_____

_____

_____

_____

_____

STUDY SUMMARY

This scripture is essential to have in your arsenal because this is an amazing song when we sing it for the right reasons, which is to remind ourselves of all the things God does for us. Praising God this way is an incredibly strong arrow of ammunition in our arsenal. Many of us only sing when we are in church following along with the choir or praise team, or when we are alone in our car listening to a tune on the radio. But using a song like this to pump up the volume of our victory is one sure way to send Satan the other way. Rock, fortress, deliverer, shield, horn, high tower, refuge, Savior, truly and yes indeed, He is worthy to be praised!

STUDY NOTES

For thou art my lamp, O Lord: and the Lord will lighten my darkness.

2nd Samuel 22:29

☐ **This Bible fact is something I know by heart.**

☐ **This Bible fact is something I need to study.**

SCRIPTURE NOTES

_____

_____

_____

_____

_____

_____

STUDY SUMMARY

This scripture is essential to have in your arsenal because when we were in the world we walked in darkness. And, unless we maintain our faith and continue to walk in the Spirit, we can sometimes slip back into darkness. Crossing back over to the dark side is what every demon wants to see in you. They want to have control of your thoughts, your imaginations, your actions, reaction, and interactions with others, so they can take credit for being the ones who made you deny God and do evil. But anytime we make mistakes, or mess up, God's light is always there are a lamp to help us find our way back to the Lord, a place where the Devil and his demons can never be again.

STUDY NOTES

_____

_____

_____

_____

_____

_____

_____

_____

_____

_____

_____

_____

Behold, happy is the man whom God correcteth: therefore despise not thou the chastening of the Almighty:

Job 5:17

☐ **This Bible fact is something I know by heart.**

☐ **This Bible fact is something I need to study.**

SCRIPTURE NOTES

_____

_____

_____

_____

_____

_____

STUDY SUMMARY

This scripture is essential to have in your arsenal because Proverbs 3:12, and Hebrews 12:6 say that God chastens those He loves. He disciplines us, prunes us, plucks and pricks us, molds us, shapes us, retools and remakes us, all for His purpose. God's plan to use us as leaders in the church and ministry cannot be accomplished without Him preparing us to be ready to meet the mission head on. And the way He does that is by correcting us, to help us learn the right way to do things, instead of us following after what we see in the world, and the actions of other people. God's way is the only way.

STUDY NOTES

_____

_____

_____

_____

_____

_____

_____

_____

_____

_____

_____

There was a man in the land of Uz, whose name was Job; and that man was perfect and upright, and one that feared God, and eschewed evil.

Job 1:1

☐ **This Bible fact is something I know by heart.**

☐ **This Bible fact is something I need to study.**

SCRIPTURE NOTES

_____

_____

_____

_____

_____

STUDY SUMMARY

This scripture is essential to have in your arsenal because every Christian at some point in our life, and often several times throughout our life, we are always asking ourselves the question of what else we can do to become more like Christ. Job was considered by God to be perfect and upright. In today's society, with all the temptations of this world, do you believe you can be perfect and upright? We see from many examples in scripture, namely Job and Jesus, that it is not only possible, but in almost every chapter in the Bible there is a reminder that we should be pursuing holiness, perfection, and righteousness, so that God will also examine us and find us just like Job and as close as we can get to Jesus.

STUDY NOTES

_____

_____

_____

_____

_____

_____

_____

_____

_____

_____

_____

He shall deliver thee in six troubles: yea, in seven there shall no evil touch thee.

Job 5:19

☐ **This Bible fact is something I know by heart.**

☐ **This Bible fact is something I need to study.**

SCRIPTURE NOTES

_____

_____

_____

_____

_____

_____

STUDY SUMMARY

This scripture is essential to have in your arsenal because the book of Job chapter fourteen verse one says *Man that is born of a woman is of few days, and full of trouble.* An old adage says *into each life some rain must fall.* In times of trouble where the Devil is busy causing chaos in our life, God wants this scripture to remind us of what He allowed the Devil to do to Job. Job lost his kids, most of his possessions, even his wife's support, but he did not falter in his faith. Job withstood the test. He did not cave in under pressure. In the end, God blessed him with double for his trouble. This verse is helpful in teaching lessons about loss and how God is the better gain.

STUDY NOTES

_____

_____

_____

_____

_____

_____

_____

_____

_____

_____

_____

In famine He shall redeem thee from death: and in war from the power of the sword. Thou shalt be hid from the scourge of the tongue: neither shalt thou be afraid of destruction when it cometh. At destruction and famine thou shalt laugh: neither shalt thou be afraid of the beasts of the earth.

Job 5:20-22

☐ **This Bible fact is something I know by heart.**

☐ **This Bible fact is something I need to study.**

SCRIPTURE NOTES

_____

_____

_____

_____

_____

_____

STUDY SUMMARY

This scripture is essential to have in your arsenal because Satan wants us to fear the things he is able to do to us. This scripture reminds us to laugh at the darts of the Devil and not to be afraid of any beast that shall come against us either physically or even in our dreams. I've had to fight numerous battles for myself as well as standing in the gap for others, in my dreams. God often sends me warnings about someone that I know immediately needs help or prayer. And, God will typically show me a vision of something that is coming my way or that others are dealing with so that I know how to fight the battle.

STUDY NOTES

_____

_____

_____

_____

_____

_____

_____

_____

_____

_____

END OF CHAPTER
READING SUGGESTION

+ Deuteronomy 6:1 to 6:25
+ Joshua 1:1 to 1:18 & 24:1 to 24:33
+ 2nd Samuel 22:1 to 22:51

The
DAGGERS

Useful for quick and immediate jabs and attacks.
Most effective when you're up close.

For thou, Lord, wilt bless the righteous; with favour wilt thou compass him as with a shield.

Psalm 5:12

☐ **This Bible fact is something I know by heart.**

☐ **This Bible fact is something I need to study.**

SCRIPTURE NOTES

_____

_____

_____

_____

_____

_____

STUDY SUMMARY

This scripture is essential to have in your arsenal because it is effective at reminding us that if we continue to pursue holiness and righteousness, that God will grant us favor and act as a shield for us against our enemies. God's blessings come in many forms. They can be for us, for our children, even our grandchildren. They can benefit those we pray for, and others we simply want to bless. Whatever the form and whichever path it takes to reach us, this scripture for teaching people that righteousness comes with the blessings of God that only He can give.

STUDY NOTES

_____

_____

_____

_____

_____

_____

_____

_____

_____

_____

_____

For thou hast girded me with strength unto the battle: thou hast subdued under me those that rose up against me. Thou hast also given me the necks of mine enemies; that I might destroy them that hate me.

Psalm 5:39-40

☐ **This Bible fact is something I know by heart.**

☐ **This Bible fact is something I need to study.**

SCRIPTURE NOTES

_____

_____

_____

_____

_____

_____

STUDY SUMMARY

This scripture is essential to have in your arsenal because people can hate you simply because of the color of your skin, your culture, your gifts, skills, talents, abilities, memory, knowledge, or resources. They can be jealous of your spouse and your children and the love they see within your family and how they see God bless you because you constantly give and share God's love with others. Enemies can do some really hateful things. This scripture is one of the ways that God continues to remind that the battle is not ours, and that He will hold us up, help us, and allow us to overcome any and every battle we will ever have to fight.

STUDY NOTES

_____

_____

_____

_____

_____

_____

_____

_____

_____

_____

_____

_____

The Lord is my rock, and my fortress, and my deliverer; my God, my strength, in whom I will trust; my buckler, and the horn of my salvation, and my high tower.

Psalm 18:2

☐ **This Bible fact is something I know by heart.**

☐ **This Bible fact is something I need to study.**

SCRIPTURE NOTES

_____

_____

_____

_____

_____

_____

STUDY SUMMARY

This scripture is essential to have in your arsenal because it is almost identical to the scripture in 2nd Samuel chapter twenty two verses one to four where David sang this as part of an amazing song. This is to further remind us of all the things God does for us. God is a Rock we can stand on; fortress we can hide inside; deliverer from every stronghold; shield from all the darts of the enemy; horn that I use to proclaim His Holy name; high tower so I can rise above my problems. I truly love the way the Bible gives us what we need when we need it, and no matter how much we eat of it, it always finds a way to feed us and help us get stronger. Use this scripture to share testimony with others of how good God has been and still is to you.

STUDY NOTES

It is God that avengeth me, and subdueth the people under me.

Psalm 18:47

☐ **This Bible fact is something I know by heart.**

☐ **This Bible fact is something I need to study.**

SCRIPTURE NOTES

_____

_____

_____

_____

_____

_____

STUDY SUMMARY

This scripture is essential to have in your arsenal because the first thing we have to be aware of going into any battle is who the General is. God is our General. He is the one who has all the strategy, and here's some reality: His strategy and plans never fail. He's never wrong. He never loses. There is no doubt about His ability, His track record, His incredible and amazing value as leader of the team. This scripture is great for teaching people that when others do us harm, God can and will fight the battle, as long as we are in His will, and doing things His way.

STUDY NOTES

_____

_____

_____

_____

_____

_____

_____

_____

_____

_____

The Lord is my shepherd; I shall not want. He maketh me to lie down in green pastures: he leadeth me beside the still waters. He restoreth my soul: he leadeth me in the paths of righteousness for his name's sake. Yea, though I walk through the valley of the shadow of death, I will fear no evil: for thou art with me; thy rod and thy staff they comfort me. Thou preparest a table before me in the presence of mine enemies: thou anointest my head with oil; my cup runneth over. Surely goodness and mercy shall follow me all the days of my life: and I will dwell in the house of the Lord for ever.

Psalm 23:1-6

☐ **This Bible fact is something I know by heart.**

☐ **This Bible fact is something I need to study.**

SCRIPTURE NOTES

_____

_____

_____

_____

_____

_____

STUDY SUMMARY

This scripture is essential to have in your arsenal because it is quite possibly one of the most memorized passages in the Bible. It's 126 words, and if we can focus our mind on memorizing this entire passage, then it should be easy for you to fix your thoughts on using your memory to memorize many or most of the Bible verses contained in this book. It's not difficult when you know that the end result is that you'll have an arsenal of ammunition to fight off any attack of the Devil.

STUDY NOTES

_____

_____

_____

_____

_____

_____

_____

_____

_____

_____

_____

The earth is the Lord's, and the fullness thereof; the world, and they that dwell therein.

Psalm 24:1

☐ This Bible fact is something I know by heart.

☐ This Bible fact is something I need to study.

SCRIPTURE NOTES

_____

_____

_____

_____

_____

_____

STUDY SUMMARY

This scripture is essential to have in your arsenal because in the wilderness when Satan tempted Jesus he used the promise of riches. Question: how do you offer to give God something He already owns!? Satan is stupid (just my opinion) for thinking that he could use trickery and temptation to try and throw Jesus off his game, knock Him off his square, and get Him to even think for a moment about doing what 1/3 of the Angels did. Question: how is it that are you an Angel, in Heaven, and you're not satisfied, to the point where you are able to be tricked into believing or convinced that the Devil, another former Angel, could overthrow God? It all belongs to Him...period.

STUDY NOTES

_____

_____

_____

_____

_____

_____

_____

_____

_____

_____

_____

The Lord is my light and my salvation; whom shall I fear? The Lord is the strength of my life; of whom shall I be afraid? When the wicked, even mine enemies and my foes, came upon me to eat up my flesh, they stumbled and fell. Though an host should encamp against me, my heart shall not fear: though war should rise against me, in this will I be confident.

Psalm 27:1-3

☐ **This Bible fact is something I know by heart.**

☐ **This Bible fact is something I need to study.**

SCRIPTURE NOTES

_____

_____

_____

_____

_____

_____

STUDY SUMMARY

This scripture is essential to have in your arsenal because over the past 20 years of my life being in church and ministry leadership I've had to face a number of battles. This scripture has always been there for me. My wife will tell you the same is true for her. Whatever we face, this passage is typically the first thing we begin to pray. Yes pray. We use this scripture as a prayer and it helps each and every single time. There are some truly evil forces in this world, and they can use people to do some hateful things. Use this scripture as both a defense mechanism and for helping you get through the fire, any time you are forced to walk into it.

STUDY NOTES

_____

_____

_____

_____

_____

_____

_____

_____

_____

_____

For in the time of trouble he shall hide me in his pavilion: in the secret of his tabernacle shall he hide me; he shall set me up upon a rock. And now shall mine head be lifted up above mine enemies round about me: therefore will I offer in his tabernacle sacrifices of joy; I will sing, yea, I will sing praises unto the Lord.

Psalm 27:5-6

☐ **This Bible fact is something I know by heart.**

☐ **This Bible fact is something I need to study.**

SCRIPTURE NOTES

_____

_____

_____

_____

_____

_____

STUDY SUMMARY

This scripture is essential to have in your arsenal because years ago I wrote a book titled *Rise Above Your Storm*. It is based on the storms that God allowed the Devil to test Job's faith with, and how in spite of all that he went through, Job did not cave in under the pressure. Instead, he rose above his storm. Because Job stood firm and stayed faithful, God blessed him with twice as much as he'd had before, including replacing the kids that Satan killed. Whatever you are going through, you can rise above it. If you need additional support, look for my book titled *Success After Setback*. It's available at major retailers and also at PastorKeith.org/books.

STUDY NOTES

_____

_____

_____

_____

_____

_____

_____

_____

_____

_____

_____

The Lord is my strength and my shield; my heart trusted in him, and I am helped: therefore my heart greatly rejoiceth; and with my song will I praise him.

Psalm 28:7

☐ **This Bible fact is something I know by heart.**

☐ **This Bible fact is something I need to study.**

SCRIPTURE NOTES

_____

_____

_____

_____

_____

_____

STUDY SUMMARY

This scripture is essential to have in your arsenal because it can help you teach people how to rejoice when they are going through and after they have made it through. My wife and I raised both our daughters in the church. We knew how important is was for them to have their lives rooted and grounded in faith, and how vital it is for them to have a relationship with God through His Son Jesus the Christ. We took them to national conventions, and group camping trips for well over ten years, and the results are a list of blessings that even this nearly 300 page book could hold. Trust in the Lord with all your heart and lean not unto your own understanding. In all your ways acknowledge Him and He will direct your paths. Rejoice and rejoice.

STUDY NOTES

_____

_____

_____

_____

_____

_____

_____

_____

_____

_____

_____

_____

For his anger endureth but a moment; in His favour is life: weeping may endure for a night, but joy cometh in the morning.

Psalm 30:5

☐ **This Bible fact is something I know by heart.**

☐ **This Bible fact is something I need to study.**

SCRIPTURE NOTES

_____

_____

_____

_____

_____

_____

STUDY SUMMARY

This scripture is essential to have in your arsenal because this is possibly another one of the most memorized and widely recognized verses in the Bible. It has been used in prayers, songs, and I've even heard it inserted into some of the lines many actors read in certain movies. Joy cometh in the morning. That in itself is reason enough for us to lay down and get some sleep. God's got it. He's still in control. He knows all. Sees all. Understands it all and is the only one who can fix it all.

STUDY NOTES

_____

_____

_____

_____

_____

_____

_____

_____

_____

_____

Let the lying lips be put to silence; which speak grievous things proudly and contemptuously against the righteous.

Psalm 31:18

☐ **This Bible fact is something I know by heart.**

☐ **This Bible fact is something I need to study.**

SCRIPTURE NOTES

_____

_____

_____

_____

_____

_____

STUDY SUMMARY

This scripture is essential to have in your arsenal because in the book of John, chapter eight, verses 42 to 44, Jesus identifies the Devil as the father of lies. As a result of this revelation, we should always tell the truth and be mindful when you know others aren't. The truth sets us free, and it is the only way that we can communicate with God and expect a response. God is not going to participate or advocate or administrate any lie that we unleash. This scripture is useful for teaching people that the Devil uses lying as a way to cause confusion. He does it in almost any situation you can imagine, and the only way to shield yourself from it, with God, is to stand on the truth.

STUDY NOTES

_____

_____

_____

_____

_____

_____

_____

_____

_____

_____

_____

The steps of a good man are ordered by the Lord: and he delighteth in his way.

Psalm 37:23

☐ **This Bible fact is something I know by heart.**

☐ **This Bible fact is something I need to study.**

SCRIPTURE NOTES

_____

_____

_____

_____

_____

_____

STUDY SUMMARY

This scripture is essential to have in your arsenal because as men and women and children of God, we have a responsibility to represent Him in a way that gives Him glory and honor and praise. This scripture is simple. It reminds us that if we do things the right way, that the Lord Himself will order our steps. And I can tell you from personal testimony that when you are walking in the way of the Lord the experience is unlike anything you can ever imagine. The scripture also says that the Lord delights in us when we are doing good.

STUDY NOTES

_____

_____

_____

_____

_____

_____

_____

_____

_____

_____

_____

I have been young, and now am old; yet have I not seen the righteous forsaken, nor his seed begging bread.

Psalm 37:25

☐ **This Bible fact is something I know by heart.**

☐ **This Bible fact is something I need to study.**

SCRIPTURE NOTES

_____

_____

_____

_____

_____

_____

STUDY SUMMARY

This scripture is essential to have in your arsenal because there are many men and women of God all over the world who have lived life and have a ton of testimony to share about how God has kept them in spite of situations that should have taken them down, or even out. I'm one of those. I've been some absolutely horrific and horrendous circumstances but no matter what I've gone through, even the thinnest of times, or the thickest of trials, God has always been there with what I needed for that moment. I've had actual interactions with Angels, on more than one occasion, which has always let me know that my life is His in more ways than I can mention.

STUDY NOTES

_____

_____

_____

_____

_____

_____

_____

_____

_____

_____

_____

Wait on the Lord, and keep his way, and He shall exalt thee to inherit the land: when the wicked are cut off, thou shalt see it.

Psalm 37:34

☐ **This Bible fact is something I know by heart.**

☐ **This Bible fact is something I need to study.**

SCRIPTURE NOTES

_____

_____

_____

_____

_____

_____

STUDY SUMMARY

This scripture is essential to have in your arsenal because often times we tend to want to rush into something that God has not opened the door for us to walk through. We have a tendency to want to move too fast, when every thing around us, all the signs, say...wait. I've been there and done that so I understand what it's like to see a vision of something and want to jump on it immediately, instead of receiving the instruction from God on how to do it and when. Only what we do for God will last. But if we jump ahead of Him, our enemies have an opportunity to steal, kill, and destroy what we're trying to build. God says when we wait on Him, He will bless us, and our enemies shall be stopped, and we will witness it.

STUDY NOTES

Through thee will we push down our enemies: through thy name will we tread them under that rise up against us.

Psalm 44:5

☐ **This Bible fact is something I know by heart.**

☐ **This Bible fact is something I need to study.**

SCRIPTURE NOTES

_____

_____

_____

_____

_____

_____

STUDY SUMMARY

This scripture is essential to have in your arsenal because it is another truly dynamic verse that confirms God's willingness to fight our battles and snuff out our enemies. That doesn't mean they will die, it means that He will move them away from us so that we can look north, south, east, and west and never again see them or be bothered by them. This is God's promise, and His word is truth. His amazing ability to act in our behalf when we are in need is something that goes without explanation. It just is. People who rise up against us, knowing that we are children of the most high God, probably don't believe they are fighting against God by fighting against you, but Moses and Pharoah are prime examples of how God will intervene on our behalf.

STUDY NOTES

_____

_____

_____

_____

_____

_____

_____

_____

_____

_____

_____

_____

God is our refuge and strength, a very present help in trouble.

Psalm 46:1

☐ **This Bible fact is something I know by heart.**

☐ **This Bible fact is something I need to study.**

SCRIPTURE NOTES

_____

_____

_____

_____

_____

_____

STUDY SUMMARY

This scripture is essential to have in your arsenal because is it yet another one of those memory verse scriptures that has been, is still being, and most likely will be deeply rooted in the church and ministry in various ways. And, whether you hear it from the pastor when He's praying or preaching, or the choir sings it in a song, this verse could not be more true in its strength. The simplicity of it is just that it contains all that anyone needs to know if they've ever had any doubt about God's ability to step in and help us when we are in trouble. God does not do this for everyone, otherwise there would never be any unsolved problems on the planet. He does it for those who love Him and are the called according to His purpose.

STUDY NOTES

_____

_____

_____

_____

_____

_____

_____

_____

_____

_____

_____

Be still, and know that I am God: I will be exalted among the heathen, I will be exalted in the Earth.

Psalm 46:10

☐ **This Bible fact is something I know by heart.**

☐ **This Bible fact is something I need to study.**

SCRIPTURE NOTES

_____

_____

_____

_____

_____

_____

STUDY SUMMARY

This scripture is essential to have in your arsenal because not only is it one of my favorite verses, it's yet another one of those scriptures that I highly recommend that you commit to memory. Anytime in the Bible where God identifies Himself, He means business. He brings the rain and the pain. He shows up in clouds by day, and pillars of fire by night. He destroys strongholds of the Devil with a single Angel killing hundreds of thousands of people who do not worship or honor Him as God. God is not mocked. He is still a just God, but also a jealous one. He created us, and He wants all the glory for it. And no matter what, He will get it, and nothing and no one will get in the way. He is an incredible friend to have and we are blessed because of it.

STUDY NOTES

_____

_____

_____

_____

_____

_____

_____

_____

_____

_____

_____

Deliver me from mine enemies, O my God: defend me from them that rise up against me.

Psalm 59:1

☐ **This Bible fact is something I know by heart.**

☐ **This Bible fact is something I need to study.**

SCRIPTURE NOTES

_____

_____

_____

_____

_____

_____

STUDY SUMMARY

This scripture is essential to have in your arsenal because I remember my first bully. His name was Eric. We were in junior high. He had me on my back on the ground one day after school, for no reason, and the entire school watched. Laying on my back, I looked up toward the sky, and the next thing I know he was on the ground and I was sitting on his chest. There is no secret to what God can do and I've seen Him do some indescribable things in an instant. It was in the blink of an eye that my situation with that bully changed, and from that moment on, I began to thank God for His presence in my life. I didn't always walk the straight and narrow, but I did always pray, and thank Him for watching over me.

STUDY NOTES

_____

_____

_____

_____

_____

_____

_____

_____

_____

_____

_____

He only is my rock and my salvation; He is my defence; I shall not be greatly moved.

Psalm 62:2

☐ **This Bible fact is something I know by heart.**

☐ **This Bible fact is something I need to study.**

SCRIPTURE NOTES

_____

_____

_____

_____

_____

_____

STUDY SUMMARY

This scripture is essential to have in your arsenal because when God's people are in trouble, He wants us to know that he is the *only one* who we should turn to for help. When we stand on His word against any type of problem or any sort of attack, God's word promises to shield us, shelter us, protect us, and defend us. I believe this because I've witnessed it happen in my own life on more than a few occasions. Each time I'm in the wrong, if I confess it, repent, ask forgiveness, and move forward knowing that I did the right thing by taking responsibility, God is right there to restore me. But anytime we carry the burden of sin without repentance, we allow demonic influences to step in and control the situation, and that is something we never want to do.

STUDY NOTES

_____

_____

_____

_____

_____

_____

_____

_____

_____

_____

Let them be ashamed and confounded that seek after my soul: let them be turned backward, and put to confusion, that desire my hurt.

Psalm 70:2

☐ **This Bible fact is something I know by heart.**

☐ **This Bible fact is something I need to study.**

SCRIPTURE NOTES

_____

_____

_____

_____

_____

_____

STUDY SUMMARY

This scripture is essential to have in your arsenal because as someone who preaches, teaches, and reaches masses of people, there are always going to be others who do not agree with or support the message, the method, or the manner in which it is distributed. Jesus gave us many examples of this and also told us that it would be so. This scripture is fantastic for showing those who are being bullied or maligned, especially across platforms like social media, that God is right there to fight the battle for us. All we have to do is be in His will, call out on His name in prayer, and He will answer us, often by sending Angels into the situation to help fight for you.

STUDY NOTES

_____

_____

_____

_____

_____

_____

_____

_____

_____

_____

_____

For the Lord God is a sun and shield: the Lord will give grace and glory: no good thing will he withhold from them that walk uprightly.

Psalm 84:11

☐ **This Bible fact is something I know by heart.**

☐ **This Bible fact is something I need to study.**

SCRIPTURE NOTES

_____

_____

_____

_____

_____

_____

STUDY SUMMARY

This scripture is essential to have in your arsenal because as I said on the previous page, when we are in the right, and in the Lord's will, we have every protection on the planet to help us. God will shield us. And He will give us all that we could ever ask or think, as long as we are in His will, and walking His way. For example, in 2013, I built and opened a bookstore/ cafe` named *Books 'N Tea*. Surrounding the space where the store operated was a drug dealer and prostitute, a person holding drunk parties daily, and a self-proclaimed warlock. All I had to do was pray, and within weeks they were all moved out of the building, and those strongholds over that space was broken, and it had stood for decades.

STUDY NOTES

_____

_____

_____

_____

_____

_____

_____

_____

_____

_____

_____

He that dwelleth in the secret place of the most High shall abide under the shadow of the Almighty. I will say of the Lord, He is my refuge and my fortress: my God; in Him will I trust. Surely he shall deliver thee from the snare of the fowler, and from the noisome pestilence. He shall cover thee with His feathers, and under His wings shalt thou trust: His truth shall be thy shield and buckler. Thou shalt not be afraid for the terror by night; nor for the arrow that flieth by day; nor for the pestilence that walketh in darkness; nor for the destruction that wasteth at noonday. A thousand shall fall at thy side, and ten thousand at thy right hand; but it shall not come nigh thee. Only with thine eyes shalt thou behold and see the reward of the wicked. Because thou hast made the Lord, which is my refuge, even the most High, thy habitation;

Psalm 91:1-9

☐ **This Bible fact is something I know by heart.**

☐ **This Bible fact is something I need to study.**

SCRIPTURE NOTES

_____

_____

_____

_____

_____

_____

STUDY SUMMARY

This scripture is essential to have in your arsenal because being able to rest in the midst of storms and enemies is the most peaceful place on the planet. God rewards the wicked for their ridicule and ridiculousness, and at the same time He shelters you from their storms. When people come at you with all sorts of attacks, and on top of that the enemy is trying to throw a wrench in your plans, God is always there to protect you. The enemy can consume your thoughts if you let him, and those who are working against you can alter your actions, if you let them. The secret is to go into your prayer closet and simply pray for those who despitefully use you and persecute you, and leave everything else to the Lord.

STUDY NOTES

_____

_____

_____

_____

_____

_____

_____

_____

_____

_____

There shall no evil befall thee, neither shall any plague come nigh thy dwelling. For he shall give His angels charge over thee, to keep thee in all thy ways. They shall bear thee up in their hands, lest thou dash thy foot against a stone. Thou shalt tread upon the lion and adder: the young lion and the dragon shalt thou trample under feet. Because he hath set his love upon me, therefore will I deliver him: I will set him on high, because he hath known my name. He shall call upon me, and I will answer him: I will be with him in trouble; I will deliver him, and honour him. With long life will I satisfy him, and shew him my salvation.

Psalm 91:10-16

☐ **This Bible fact is something I know by heart.**

☐ **This Bible fact is something I need to study.**

SCRIPTURE NOTES

_____

_____

_____

_____

_____

STUDY SUMMARY

This scripture is essential to have in your arsenal because when God blew His breath on the words written down by men as examples for how we should interact with God and His people, God meant it as a gesture of good will toward all men. Every act of God is a miracle simply because He does not have to do any of it. He is God all by Himself. There is no one like Him. He operates at a level that we can never understand. He lives in a light that no man can approach. His ways are higher than our ways. His thoughts are higher than our thoughts. He never sleeps nor slumbers. He cannot sin or lie. There is no darkness in Him. All of this and more He uses to protect us including Angels who still love, honor, and serve Him.

STUDY NOTES

_____

_____

_____

_____

_____

_____

_____

_____

_____

_____

_____

_____

Make a joyful noise unto the Lord, all ye lands. Serve the Lord with gladness: come before his presence with singing. Know ye that the Lord he is God: it is He that hath made us, and not we ourselves; we are His people, and the sheep of His pasture. Enter into His gates with thanksgiving, and into His courts with praise: be thankful unto Him, and bless His name. For the Lord is good; His mercy is everlasting; and His truth endureth to all generations.

Psalm 100:1-5

☐ **This Bible fact is something I know by heart.**

☐ **This Bible fact is something I need to study.**

SCRIPTURE NOTES

_____

_____

_____

_____

_____

STUDY SUMMARY

This scripture is essential to have in your arsenal because it reminds me of a lesson I taught titled *Introduction to Prayer*. You can find it as slideshow and video #60 at PastorKeith.org/videos or as a Podcast in audio format as #01 at PastorKeith.org in the Podcast section. In the lesson I teach that the way to stay in communication with God is to first enter into His gates with Thanksgiving and into His courts with praise. I show in detail several ways to do this. As the sheep of His pasture, we expect to be led, to be fed, to be nurtured, and to be protected from the wolves of the world. And as long as we serve the Lord He will lead us with His mighty hand.

STUDY NOTES

_____

_____

_____

_____

_____

_____

_____

_____

_____

_____

_____

O give thanks unto the Lord; for He is good: because His mercy endureth for ever.

Psalm 118:1

☐ **This Bible fact is something I know by heart.**

☐ **This Bible fact is something I need to study.**

SCRIPTURE NOTES

_____

_____

_____

_____

_____

STUDY SUMMARY

This scripture is essential to have in your arsenal because where else can you find a God who will give you mercy for things you've messed up, and do so constantly and consistently, no matter what you've done? God is most certainly good. His platform and the foundation of goodness that He sits on have been passed on to us as a way for us to rise up above any and every possible obstacle that could come against us. We are to teach people that no matter what this opposition does to us, we are to stay on the battlefield for the Lord and do our very best to constantly remind one another to praise and thank God for His goodness and His mercy because we can never find them anywhere else.

STUDY NOTES

_____

_____

_____

_____

_____

_____

_____

_____

_____

_____

_____

The Lord is on my side; I will not fear: what can man do unto me?

Psalm 118:6

☐ This Bible fact is something I know by heart.

☐ This Bible fact is something I need to study.

SCRIPTURE NOTES

_____

_____

_____

_____

_____

STUDY SUMMARY

This scripture is essential to have in your arsenal because it speaks to the very heart of why it is that no enemy including Satan, sin, demons, dragons and even the dungeons they reside in, can come against God's people and be victorious. I didn't say that the attacks wouldn't come, I said that they would not prevail over you as long as you stand and believe that this and all other scriptures that give you boldness in the battle, can and will hold you up and protect you from any and all harm. God is a man of His word. He speaks it and it happens. He wills it and it comes to pass. That should be all you need for yourself, and to teach others who need strength the very fact of the scripture: *what can man do unto you!?*

STUDY NOTES

_____

_____

_____

_____

_____

_____

_____

_____

_____

_____

_____

I will lift up mine eyes unto the hills, from whence cometh my help. My help cometh from the Lord, which made Heaven and Earth.

Psalm 121:1-2

☐ **This Bible fact is something I know by heart.**

☐ **This Bible fact is something I need to study.**

SCRIPTURE NOTES

_____

_____

_____

_____

_____

_____

STUDY SUMMARY

This scripture is essential to have in your arsenal because amazingly this is yet another one of the most popular prayers, song lyric, and memory verse that is still today, in 2016, helping people as it says it will. When you are at a place in your life where you see the darkness of the world becoming more than you can digest, lift up your eyes unto the hills, because your help is right there waiting for you. Our help comes from the Lord, who indeed has made Heaven and Earth. It is our responsibility to remember this, remind others of it, and recall it any and every time the Devil wants to plant seeds of doubt in your mind about materialism or mess.

STUDY NOTES

_____

_____

_____

_____

_____

_____

_____

_____

_____

_____

_____

If it had not been the Lord who was on our side, when men rose up against us:

Psalm 124:2

☐ **This Bible fact is something I know by heart.**

☐ **This Bible fact is something I need to study.**

SCRIPTURE NOTES

_____

_____

_____

_____

_____

STUDY SUMMARY

This scripture is essential to have in your arsenal because again, the first of this verse is yet another one of the most popular, memorized, sung, taught, and recited through personal testimony. I can testify that *if it had not been for the Lord on my side* I would have been dead and gone. I was born in Chicago and raised on the south side in the Englewood community where most of the violence and death is still taking place today. Gangs, guns, drugs, and jail was a part of life until I got sick and tired of being sick and tired, met the woman who has been by side for the past 32 years, and followed God's lead to leave that life behind, in exchange for peace that passeth all measure of understanding, which we found by raising our kids in Minnesota.

STUDY NOTES

_____

_____

_____

_____

_____

_____

_____

_____

_____

_____

_____

Blessed be the Lord my strength, which teacheth my hands to war, and my fingers to fight: my goodness, and my fortress; my high tower, and my deliverer; my shield, and He in whom I trust;

Psalm 144:1-2

☐ **This Bible fact is something I know by heart.**

☐ **This Bible fact is something I need to study.**

SCRIPTURE NOTES

_____

_____

_____

_____

_____

STUDY SUMMARY

This scripture is essential to have in your arsenal because as it says, the Lord is Him who teaches us how to war and fight. We don't come out of the womb with the knowledge of how to defeat the enemy, but we do have an enemy the moment we exit the womb. The Bible says that we are born into sin and shaped in iniquity. We have to learn, with the teaching of Jesus Christ, how to navigate the landscape of life so that we can not only fight the battle, but win the war. Satan is never going to stop sending soldiers who follow him, after us. Their opposition will always be a part of our life until either we are laid to rest, raptured away from this planet, or Revelation 20:10, which details the Devil's end, comes to pass.

STUDY NOTES

_____

_____

_____

_____

_____

_____

_____

_____

_____

_____

_____

END OF CHAPTER
READING SUGGESTION

+ The entire book of the Psalm
Psalm 1:1 to 150:6
One chapter per day should take five months.

The
DRONES

When attacking from a distance you need to use wisdom knowledge, understanding and prophecy.

Happy is the man that findeth wisdom, and the man that getteth understanding. For the merchandise of it is better than the merchandise of silver, and the gain thereof than fine gold. She is more precious than rubies: and all the things thou canst desire are not to be compared unto her. Length of days is in her right hand; and in her left hand riches and honour. Her ways are ways of pleasantness, and all her paths are peace. She is a tree of life to them that lay hold upon her: and happy is every one that retaineth her.

Proverbs 3:13-18

☐ **This Bible fact is something I know by heart.**

☐ **This Bible fact is something I need to study.**

SCRIPTURE NOTES

_____

_____

_____

_____

_____

STUDY SUMMARY

This scripture is essential to have in your arsenal because as these wonderful words of wisdom says that if you find wisdom, and get understanding, that happiness is attached to them. It adds that the benefits of it are better than even the highest quality of gold and rubies, and anything we possibly desire cannot be measured against it. It contains longevity and wealth and respect and tranquility and a source of sustainability. I find this scripture useful for teaching about how to de-stress your life and to stop sweating the small stuff. This is an incredible statement to make, but because God is who He is, He knows He can make it because He's the only one who can back it up.

STUDY NOTES

_____

_____

_____

_____

_____

_____

_____

_____

_____

_____

_____

When a man's ways please the Lord, He maketh even his enemies to be at peace with him.

Proverbs 16:7

☐ **This Bible fact is something I know by heart.**

☐ **This Bible fact is something I need to study.**

SCRIPTURE NOTES

_____

_____

_____

_____

_____

_____

STUDY SUMMARY

This scripture is essential to have in your arsenal because this is possibly one of the most effective scriptures for teaching how to have peace within any storm. God can make our enemies to be at peace with us!? Wow! Knowing that this is possible, doesn't it make you want to make sure that everything you do in life pleases the Lord? Doesn't it make you want to walk right, talk right, sing and pray right, live right, love right, and do any and everything you can to teach others how to do the same once you've achieved it? Doesn't it make you want to live it so that you will never have to worry about having your enemies at war with you? That in itself is enough motivation to live right.

STUDY NOTES

_____

_____

_____

_____

_____

_____

_____

_____

_____

_____

_____

_____

If thine enemy be hungry, give him bread to eat; and if he be thirsty, give him water to drink: For thou shalt heap coals of fire upon his head, and the Lord shall reward thee.

Proverbs 25:21-22

☐ This Bible fact is something I know by heart.

☐ This Bible fact is something I need to study.

SCRIPTURE NOTES

_____

_____

_____

_____

_____

STUDY SUMMARY

This scripture is essential to have in your arsenal because it is one of the most difficult things to do in battle, which is to make a sacrifice to ensure that your enemy is served. I've been in situations where I had to swallow my words and hold my peace, cook for and serve food and drink to my enemy, just because this is one of my favorite scriptures. The second half of this verse speaks to what God will do for you if you keep the peace, and if you sacrifice and serve, but it speaks volumes about what God will do *to* your enemy if you do these things. I'm a living witness that God will fight your battles in a way that makes you stronger in the end.

STUDY NOTES

_____

_____

_____

_____

_____

_____

_____

_____

_____

_____

_____

_____

How art thou fallen from Heaven, O Lucifer, son of the morning! How art thou cut down to the ground, which didst weaken the nations!

Isaiah 14:12

☐ **This Bible fact is something I know by heart.**

☐ **This Bible fact is something I need to study.**

SCRIPTURE NOTES

_____

_____

_____

_____

_____

_____

STUDY SUMMARY

This scripture is essential to have in your arsenal because this verse reminds Satan of his fall from grace. He was in Heaven, near God, as an anointed cherub, more beautiful than all the others, because he was adorned with all types of jewels. The book of Ezekiel chapter 28 tells most of the story about his eviction from Heaven but it was because wickedness was found in his heart and iniquity became his inspiration and malice became his motivation. He did so much damage that he was able to convince a third of the Angels who were in Heaven at that time, before God formed the Earth and created man, Lucifer convinced a third of the Angels, to follow his plan to overthrow God. They failed miserably, were all kicked out of glory, and banished to Earth to await their eventual end, which is eternity in Hell.

STUDY NOTES

_____

_____

_____

_____

_____

_____

_____

_____

_____

_____

But they that wait upon the Lord shall renew their strength; they shall mount up with wings as eagles; they shall run, and not be weary; and they shall walk, and not faint.

Isaiah 40:31

☐ **This Bible fact is something I know by heart.**

☐ **This Bible fact is something I need to study.**

SCRIPTURE NOTES

_____

_____

_____

_____

_____

STUDY SUMMARY

This scripture is essential to have in your arsenal because it is another verse that you should commit to memory so that when attacks do come, you will not be tempted to respond before it is your time to do so. Waiting for God's direction and protection gives you many benefits in battle. First and certainly foremost is the fact that God Himself says that waiting renews your strength; and doing so will enable you to rise above your storm; stay in the battle without getting tired; and no matter what you go through, you shall walk upright without getting tired. God is an awesome God and this scripture is useful for teaching these and other critical facts.

STUDY NOTES

_____

_____

_____

_____

_____

_____

_____

_____

_____

_____

_____

But thus saith the Lord, even the captives of the mighty shall be taken away, and the prey of the terrible shall be delivered: for I will contend with him that contendeth with thee, and I will save thy children.

Isaiah 49:25

☐ **This Bible fact is something I know by heart.**

☐ **This Bible fact is something I need to study.**

SCRIPTURE NOTES

_____

_____

_____

_____

_____

_____

STUDY SUMMARY

This scripture is essential to have in your arsenal because at the moment you begin believing in the power of God's word to protect you against all of your adversaries and their attacks, you have learned to believe and trust in God. The battle is not yours. God says that He will come up against those who come against you. He will say not only you but your children too! This is an incredible way to teach new members how to learn to trust in God and lean not unto their own understanding, and that if they simple acknowledge Him He will see to it that His word comes to pass each and every single time. We must be mindful, however, that this only works for those of us who are living right and are in His will.

STUDY NOTES

_____

_____

_____

_____

_____

_____

_____

_____

_____

_____

_____

No weapon that is formed against thee shall prosper; and every tongue that shall rise against thee in judgment thou shalt condemn. This is the heritage of the servants of the Lord, and their righteousness is of me, saith the Lord.

Isaiah 54:17

☐ **This Bible fact is something I know by heart.**

☐ **This Bible fact is something I need to study.**

SCRIPTURE NOTES

_____

_____

_____

_____

_____

_____

STUDY SUMMARY

This scripture is essential to have in your arsenal because this is the verse I've used on the battlefield for many years. It's the first thing I think of when I see or hear of an attack coming my way, and it is the one I keep in my own arsenal no matter when I travel, what I teach, or where I preach. This verse is at the top of the list for being one of the most memorized and referred to in sermons and songs, and has become a banner cry for many people who know it by heart and understand its power. It has proven technique and strategy contained within it that will help you no matter what you are going through and you should always remember to teach this to others as well.

STUDY NOTES

_____

_____

_____

_____

_____

_____

_____

_____

_____

_____

So shall they fear the name of the Lord from the west, and His glory from the rising of the sun. When the enemy shall come in like a flood, the Spirit of the Lord shall lift up a standard against him.

Isaiah 59:19

☐ **This Bible fact is something I know by heart.**

☐ **This Bible fact is something I need to study.**

SCRIPTURE NOTES

_____

_____

_____

_____

_____

_____

STUDY SUMMARY

This scripture is essential to have in your arsenal because since I was age 17, my life has been one very long battle against an enemy I know has been and still is determined that I never make it to my destiny. There have been so many attacks that I cannot list them all as it would take an entire volume of encyclopedias to even get started. I used to think that I was crazy or even confused about the things that were taking place in my life, especially when I started hearing that no one else was experiencing the same level of war that I have been all those times. But it was after praying to God one day when two Angels showed up, invisible to the human eye, and talked to me in my mind, without me opening my mouth, just to answer my prayer. It was then that I knew why the Devil has been trying to stop me all these years.

STUDY NOTES

_____

_____

_____

_____

_____

_____

_____

_____

_____

_____

Before I formed thee in the belly I knew thee; and before thou camest forth out of the womb I sanctified thee, and I ordained thee a prophet unto the nations. Then said I, Ah, Lord GOD! behold, I cannot speak: for I am a child. But the Lord said unto me, Say not, I am a child: for thou shalt go to all that I shall send thee, and whatsoever I command thee thou shalt speak. Be not afraid of their faces: for I am with thee to deliver thee, saith the Lord. Then the Lord put forth his hand, and touched my mouth. And the Lord said unto me, Behold, I have put my words in thy mouth. See, I have this day set thee over the nations and over the kingdoms, to root out, and to pull down, and to destroy, and to throw down, to build, and to plant.

Jeremiah 1:5-10

☐ **This Bible fact is something I know by heart.**

☐ **This Bible fact is something I need to study.**

SCRIPTURE NOTES

_____

_____

_____

_____

_____

_____

STUDY SUMMARY

This scripture is essential to have in your arsenal because if you've ever had any doubt about your calling or wondered why God chose you to carry His message and represent Him in the church and in the ministry, this scripture should help you, and should help you teach others too. God knows how and why He created you; ordained you; sanctified you; and put His word in you. God wants us to represent Him in the battle. He wants us to work hard to destroy the Devil's strongholds in the lives of people who love God and are the called according to His purpose. He wants us to be the ones who plant victory in some and simply stop by to water others, so He can give them His increase, and He can get the glory.

STUDY NOTES

_____

_____

_____

_____

_____

_____

_____

_____

_____

_____

END OF CHAPTER
READING SUGGESTION

+ The entire book of Proverbs
One chapter per day should take you a month.

The MINES

Meant to be planted where they will damage enemy strongholds when he least expects it.

Son of man, say unto the prince of Tyrus, thus saith the Lord God; Because thine heart is lifted up, and thou hast said, I am a God, I sit in the seat of God, in the midst of the seas; yet thou art a man, and not God, though thou set thine heart as the heart of God:

Ezekiel 28:2

☐ **This Bible fact is something I know by heart.**

☐ **This Bible fact is something I need to study.**

SCRIPTURE NOTES

_____

_____

_____

_____

_____

STUDY SUMMARY

This scripture is essential to have in your arsenal because Satan's fall from grace was not by happenstance. It was a planned power move on the part of God to eradicate Heaven of the Devil and all his new demons. You may ask yourself how Angels could have been convinced to corrupt themselves and collude with the enemy to try and overthrow the Kingdom of God. How could people who were in paradise, enjoying the love of God in eternity, ever allow themselves to be broadsided into believing that Satan's plan to take over would ever work? This scripture, starts telling the story of Satan's downfall, and it is one you should use to constantly remind him of it each and every chance you get. It keeps him off your back because he doesn't like being reminded of how God broke his back.

STUDY NOTES

_____

_____

_____

_____

_____

_____

_____

_____

_____

_____

Therefore thus saith the Lord God; Because thou hast set thine heart as the heart of God; Behold, therefore I will bring strangers upon thee, the terrible of the nations: and they shall draw their swords against the beauty of thy wisdom, and they shall defile thy brightness.

Ezekiel 28:6-7

☐ **This Bible fact is something I know by heart.**

☐ **This Bible fact is something I need to study.**

SCRIPTURE NOTES

_____

_____

_____

_____

_____

_____

STUDY SUMMARY

This scripture is essential to have in your arsenal because this part of the war in Heaven story speaks directly to why God eventually made the first of the Ten Commandments that were given to man, *thou shalt have no other gods before me*. The experience of having to cleanse Heaven of the cult-like following of Angels God had anointed and allowed access to Heaven, all because one of them wanted to be God instead of being satisfied with serving, worshiping and living with God had to be very difficult for God. It has always made me wonder whether the actions of the Devil and those who have now become demons, hurt God in any way. Satan was foolish to think he could accomplish what he set out to do, which is the reason he is so angry with man, and continues to take it out on us who he sees as receiving the promise to be given the salvation he lost.

STUDY NOTES

_____

_____

_____

_____

_____

_____

_____

_____

_____

_____

They shall bring thee down to the pit, and thou shalt die the deaths of them that are slain in the midst of the seas.

Ezekiel 28:8

☐ This Bible fact is something I know by heart.

☐ This Bible fact is something I need to study.

SCRIPTURE NOTES

_____

_____

_____

_____

_____

_____

STUDY SUMMARY

This scripture is essential to have in your arsenal because further into the story of how Satan fell from grace God allows us to see part of the start of the punishment He inflicts on the Devil. God is not mocked. His rules and regulations for living apply to Earth, Heaven, and Eternity. Anyone who chooses to take it upon themselves to break the rules will suffer under the punishment for breaking them. The Bible says that the wages of sin is death. This means that the penalty for sin, which is death, without true confession, repentance, forgiveness, and redemption, wrapped in the goodness of grace and mercy, is what we can expect when we commit sin. God allows us to see what happened the Devil sinned, and as the story goes, his life shall come to and end as detailed in Revelation 20:10.

STUDY NOTES

_____

_____

_____

_____

_____

_____

_____

_____

Thou hast been in Eden the garden of God; every precious stone was thy covering, the sardius, topaz, and the diamond, the beryl, the onyx, and the jasper, the sapphire, the emerald, and the carbuncle, and gold: the workmanship of thy tabrets and of thy pipes was prepared in thee in the day that thou wast created. Thou art the anointed cherub that covereth; and I have set thee so: thou wast upon the holy mountain of God; thou hast walked up and down in the midst of the stones of fire. Thou wast perfect in thy ways from the day that thou wast created, till iniquity was found in thee.

Ezekiel 28:13-15

☐   **This Bible fact is something I know by heart.**

☐   **This Bible fact is something I need to study.**

SCRIPTURE NOTES

_____

_____

_____

_____

_____

_____

STUDY SUMMARY

This scripture is essential to have in your arsenal because this is the passage that paves the way for the rest of the story about the Devil's downfall. As one of the anointed cherubs, Lucifer was wisdom far above others, and he was set apart by being adorned with precious gems. The Bible says he was *perfect*. God was so proud of the workmanship he put into creating Lucifer that he has spend much time explaining it. I'm currently working on a couple of book and film projects that speak directly to this issue so that they can be used as teaching tools. (1) *Cross Man Comics* is a series devoted to the Cross Man team doing battle with and defeating the enemy. (2) *Faith In Film* is a show that uses interview sessions with Hollywood stars to get their inside information and insight into the industry. Both are scheduled to launch in late 2016 early 2017. More information available soon at PastorKeith.org.

STUDY NOTES

_____

_____

_____

_____

_____

_____

_____

_____

_____

_____

By the multitude of thy merchandise they have filled the midst of thee with violence, and thou hast sinned: therefore I will cast thee as profane out of the mountain of God: and I will destroy thee, O covering cherub, from the midst of the stones of fire. Thine heart was lifted up because of thy beauty, thou hast corrupted thy wisdom by reason of thy brightness: I will cast thee to the ground, I will lay thee before kings, that they may behold thee.

Ezekiel 28:16-17

☐ **This Bible fact is something I know by heart.**

☐ **This Bible fact is something I need to study.**

SCRIPTURE NOTES

_____

_____

_____

_____

_____

_____

STUDY SUMMARY

This scripture is essential to have in your arsenal because going even deeper into the story, God says the Devil became distracted with how beautiful he was; he became materialistic; and his penalty and punishment was final. First, he was cast out of Heaven with all those he corrupted. Then God says that everyone in leadership on Earth will see Satan's demise. This story and all the passages that accompany it, is indescribable for teaching both children and adults the front end of salvation from the sin perspective. Satan ended up in the Garden of Eden on Earth, and was there before man was created, which is when he saw the opportunity to get back at God for being exiled. And even though he managed to set Adam and Eve on a course that got them both evicted from the Garden, God made the decision to send Jesus so that the sins of the people living in this lost and dying world would end.

STUDY NOTES

_____

_____

_____

_____

_____

_____

_____

_____

_____

_____

Thou hast defiled thy sanctuaries by the multitude of thine iniquities, by the iniquity of thy traffick; therefore will I bring forth a fire from the midst of thee, it shall devour thee, and I will bring thee to ashes upon the Earth in the sight of all them that behold thee.

Ezekiel 28:18

☐ **This Bible fact is something I know by heart.**

☐ **This Bible fact is something I need to study.**

SCRIPTURE NOTES

_____

_____

_____

_____

_____

_____

STUDY SUMMARY

This scripture is essential to have in your arsenal because it brings the story of Satan's sadness home. The Devil began to traffic in sin. Iniquity became his commodity and he sold this bill of goods to a third of the Angels in Heaven. What is most amazing to me about this entire scenario is that God is not at all keeping us from knowing it. In fact, he published it so that it would serve as a reminder for anyone thinking about trying to follow in Satan's foolish footsteps. I cannot imagine anyone, especially Angels, being in Heaven with almighty God, not being content and satisfied living for all eternity with God. It's the one thing most if not all Christians want the most, so for someone to have it and then lost it, is reason enough to stay the course so we won't miss our opportunity for salvation, and have it taken from us.

STUDY NOTES

_____

_____

_____

_____

_____

_____

_____

_____

_____

_____

All they that know thee among the people shall be astonished at thee: thou shalt be a terror, and never shalt thou be any more.

Ezekiel 28:19

☐ This Bible fact is something I know by heart.

☐ This Bible fact is something I need to study.

SCRIPTURE NOTES

_____

_____

_____

_____

_____

STUDY SUMMARY

This scripture is essential to have in your arsenal because again, God has not kept us from knowing the story behind the Devil's downfall, and seeing how God plans to deal with it once and for all. God's anger kindled against Satan to the point where he will be making a mockery of him at his eventual end. The book of Revelation tells the end of the story, but back in the Old Testament, the book of Ezekiel has the outline, the detail, and the determination of God to put an end to what happened. When Jesus came to Earth, His story tells and shows us how He acted, reacted, and interacted whenever He encountered demons. Jesus would call them out, then cast them out. This scripture is useful for teaching people hope behind the Hell most of us go through in our lives.

STUDY NOTES

_____

_____

_____

_____

_____

_____

_____

_____

_____

_____

And he shewed me Joshua the high priest standing before the angel of the LORD, and Satan standing at his right hand to resist him. And the Lord said unto Satan, The Lord rebuke thee, O Satan; even the Lord that hath chosen Jerusalem rebuke thee: is not this a brand plucked out of the fire? Now Joshua was clothed with filthy garments, and stood before the angel. And he answered and spake unto those that stood before him, saying, Take away the filthy garments from him. And unto him he said, Behold, I have caused thine iniquity to pass from thee, and I will clothe thee with change of raiment. And I said, let them set a fair mitre upon his head. So they set a fair mitre upon his head, and clothed him with garments. And the angel of the Lord stood by. And the angel of the LORD protested unto Joshua, saying, thus saith the LORD of hosts; If thou wilt walk in my ways, and if thou wilt keep my charge, then thou shalt also judge my house, and shalt also keep my courts, and I will give thee places to walk among these that stand by. Hear now, O Joshua the high priest, thou, and thy fellows that sit before thee: for they are men wondered at: for, behold, I will bring forth my servant the BRANCH. For behold the stone that I have laid before Joshua; upon one stone shall be seven eyes: behold, I will engrave the graving thereof, saith the Lord of hosts, and I will remove the iniquity of that land in one day.

Zechariah 3:1-9

☐ **This Bible fact is something I know by heart.**

☐ **This Bible fact is something I need to study.**

SCRIPTURE NOTES

_____

_____

_____

_____

_____

STUDY SUMMARY

This scripture is essential to have in your arsenal because this is another very interesting story that details how Satan's plans are always destroyed by the Lord. In this passage, Satan is in the role as prosecutor when Joshua is brought before God to be judged on the things he did in his life. You can read the story for yourself, but you'll find that the Lord is not moved by the Devil's attempts to attack the people who have chosen to follow Him. Joshua was blessed abundantly and this scripture is one more way to teach people how to have faith in the fire.

STUDY NOTES

_____

_____

_____

_____

_____

_____

_____

_____

_____

_____

_____

Not by might, nor by power, but by my Spirit, saith the Lord of hosts.

Zechariah 4:6

☐ **This Bible fact is something I know by heart.**

☐ **This Bible fact is something I need to study.**

SCRIPTURE NOTES

_____

_____

_____

_____

_____

_____

STUDY SUMMARY

This scripture is essential to have in your arsenal because when God sends Angels to build a hedge of protection around us, and to intervene in our life against our adversaries, and to use the Holy Spirit to help us confidently walk into our calling and pursue our purpose. Even some of the most well learned Christians may have difficulty doing this. God says that it's not by our might, or by any power we could ever hope to obtain, but it is His Spirit that gives us exactly what we need when we need it. Faith in God gives us the boldness to drive into our destiny and not continue to look back over our shoulder to see if anything in our past will ever catch us. When God closes doors to the past, He opens new ones for our future.

STUDY NOTES

_____

_____

_____

_____

_____

_____

_____

_____

_____

_____

END OF CHAPTER
READING SUGGESTION

+ Ezekiel chapter 28 and Zechariah chapters 3 and 4

The
MISSILES

Capable of destroying the enemy from anywhere at anytime.
Considered the strongest of all the weapons.

Blessed are the poor in spirit: for their's is the kingdom of heaven. Blessed are they that mourn: for they shall be comforted. Blessed are the meek: for they shall inherit the earth. Blessed are they which do hunger and thirst after righteousness: for they shall be filled. Blessed are the merciful: for they shall obtain mercy. Blessed are the pure in heart: for they shall see God. Blessed are the peacemakers: for they shall be called the children of God. Blessed are they which are persecuted for righteousness' sake: for their's is the kingdom of heaven. Blessed are ye, when men shall revile you, and persecute you, and shall say all manner of evil against you falsely, for my sake.

Matthew 5:3-11

☐ **This Bible fact is something I know by heart.**

☐ **This Bible fact is something I need to study.**

SCRIPTURE NOTES

_____

_____

_____

_____

_____

_____

STUDY SUMMARY

This scripture is essential to have in your arsenal because this passage is considered the Beatitudes. It seems to me to be a manifesto of Heaven; an instruction manual of sorts. It's the sermon on the mount, which is widely considered one of Jesus' most popular sermons. It may have been his first after completing His 40 day and 40 night Fast. From the look of things, it seems Jesus was pouring out His heart to those who would listen. These words show His passion and His love for us. This is an incredibly rare look into the heart of The King, our Lord and Savior Jesus the Christ. Use this scripture to teach people exactly what it says, as the power is in the words.

STUDY NOTES

_____

_____

_____

_____

_____

_____

_____

_____

_____

_____

_____

Ye have heard that it hath been said, Thou shalt love thy neighbour, and hate thine enemy. But I say unto you, Love your enemies, bless them that curse you, do good to them that hate you, and pray for them which despitefully use you, and persecute you;

Matthew 5:43-44

☐ **This Bible fact is something I know by heart.**

☐ **This Bible fact is something I need to study.**

SCRIPTURE NOTES

_____

_____

_____

_____

_____

_____

STUDY SUMMARY

This scripture is essential to have in your arsenal because while this may indeed be one of the most popular scriptures for fighting any battle, it may be one of the most difficult for us to use. Loving our enemies is not a natural action. Praying for our adversaries is not a natural reaction. We typically want God to punish them for hurting us. The next verse after this passage sums up the passage, which says *That ye may be the children of your Father which is in heaven: for he maketh his sun to rise on the evil and on the good, and sendeth rain on the just and on the unjust.* This comes while Jesus is teaching how to respond to attacks. I encourage you to read and teach this *entire* chapter five of Matthew.

STUDY NOTES

_____

_____

_____

_____

_____

_____

_____

_____

_____

_____

And when thou prayest, thou shalt not be as the hypocrites are: for they love to pray standing in the synagogues and in the corners of the streets, that they may be seen of men. Verily I say unto you, They have their reward. But thou, when thou prayest, enter into thy closet, and when thou hast shut thy door, pray to thy Father which is in secret; and thy Father which seeth in secret shall reward thee openly. But when ye pray, use not vain repetitions, as the heathen do: for they think that they shall be heard for their much speaking. Be not ye therefore like unto them: for your Father knoweth what things ye have need of, before ye ask him. After this manner therefore pray ye: Our Father which art in heaven, Hallowed be thy name. Thy kingdom come. Thy will be done in earth, as it is in Heaven. Give us this day our daily bread. And forgive us our debts, as we forgive our debtors. And lead us not into temptation, but deliver us from evil: For thine is the kingdom, and the power, and the glory, for ever. Amen.

Matthew 6:5-13

☐ **This Bible fact is something I know by heart.**

☐ **This Bible fact is something I need to study.**

SCRIPTURE NOTES

_____

_____

_____

_____

_____

STUDY SUMMARY

This scripture is essential to have in your arsenal because it is the roadmap for prayer. I've prayed inside a closed room for many, many years. I know that I'm most effective doing it this way. I've followed the protocol and in doing so I see results more often than when I pray any other way. There is something about being alone in a room with God when no one else is there. There is an unveiling of sorts, whereas I'm completely exposed down to my rawness and nakedness, even if I have clothes on. I'm wide open when I pray this way and I believe, and know from personal experience, that it is the only way that I can get the most heartfelt prayers through. Teach prayer to your students, other saints, and your staff. I suggest the movie *War Room* as it is an incredible way to show why praying this way is important.

STUDY NOTES

_____

_____

_____

_____

_____

_____

_____

_____

_____

_____

Moreover when ye fast, be not, as the hypocrites, of a sad countenance: for they disfigure their faces, that they may appear unto men to fast. Verily I say unto you, They have their reward. But thou, when thou fastest, anoint thine head, and wash thy face; that thou appear not unto men to fast, but unto thy Father which is in secret: and thy Father, which seeth in secret, shall reward thee openly.

Matthew 6:16-18

☐ **This Bible fact is something I know by heart.**

☐ **This Bible fact is something I need to study.**

SCRIPTURE NOTES

_____

_____

_____

_____

_____

STUDY SUMMARY

This scripture is essential to have in your arsenal because I'm someone who believes strongly in the power of Fasting. I believe in it so strongly that I do it as often as I can. If I could always Fast, and only eat when I absolutely needed to, I would live my life this way. I recently completed a 40-day Fast. It was one of the most amazing experiences I've ever gone through. To give people a glimpse into what I went through, I wrote a book about the journey as a journal that others can use to document your own. The book is titled *Fasting For Change* and you can find it at major retailers such as Amazon, Barnes & Noble, and Bookwire. Or, look for it in the New Release section at PastorKeith.org. Fasting helps strengthen God's Spirit is us over our flesh that the Devil tries to use against us. This is why it's so vitally important to me to Fast regularly. Teach others this scripture and the sacrifice.

STUDY NOTES

_____

_____

_____

_____

_____

_____

_____

_____

_____

But seek ye first the kingdom of God, and His righteousness; and all these things shall be added unto you.

Matthew 6:33

☐ **This Bible fact is something I know by heart.**

☐ **This Bible fact is something I need to study.**

SCRIPTURE NOTES

_____

_____

_____

_____

_____

_____

STUDY SUMMARY

This scripture is essential to have in your arsenal because it is another very popular memory verse, but also a roadmap of sorts for how God's blessings can come upon us. This scripture speaks volumes in terms of our wants and toward the *things* we chase after. God is implying that He's not against us having certain things, He's more concerned about them having us. He wants us to have *no* other gods before Him. And unfortunately, many of us are guilty of allowing things such as money get in between our relationship with God. We tend to seek after things instead of the creator of those things. This scripture is very helpful for reminding us what is more important overall.

STUDY NOTES

_____

_____

_____

_____

_____

_____

_____

_____

_____

_____

_____

And He called unto him the twelve, and began to send them forth by two and two; and gave them power over unclean spirits;

Mark 6:7

☐ **This Bible fact is something I know by heart.**

☐ **This Bible fact is something I need to study.**

SCRIPTURE NOTES

_____

_____

_____

_____

_____

_____

STUDY SUMMARY

This scripture is essential to have in your arsenal because Jesus set the standard and gave us the example for how to leave the four walls of our cushy, comfortable, church pews, and go out during the week to feed, clothe, visit, minister, and help. His example is simple: after three years of training within your church, you should be ready to go out and represent your church in these areas of ministry. While most certainly there are other areas of ministry that need attention, this list is what Jesus Himself set as a standard for many things including getting to Heaven, and for church growth while on Earth. If we simply follow His plan, going out two by two, we will be amazed at how much of an impact we can make. As an added bonus, consider all the wonderful testimony that will be brought back and reported to the church!

STUDY NOTES

_____

_____

_____

_____

_____

_____

_____

_____

_____

And they went out, and preached that men should repent. And they cast out many devils, and anointed with oil many that were sick, and healed them.

Mark 6:12-13

☐ **This Bible fact is something I know by heart.**

☐ **This Bible fact is something I need to study.**

SCRIPTURE NOTES

_____

_____

_____

_____

_____

_____

STUDY SUMMARY

This scripture is essential to have in your arsenal because in addition to the wonderful testimony mentioned on the previous page, think of all the people you'll be able to witness to, and minister to, and spread love and joy to. In these last and evil days, the fruit of the Spirit and the free gift of salvation are more important than ever. Why? Because once the rapture happens, there won't be a chance for those who didn't accept them to do so any longer. The time is short, and that time is now. Carrying this message, even if you don't use anything else, is vitally important as a way to lift up Jesus so He can draw people unto Himself. His welcome into the Kingdom of God will eventually come to an end because the door will close...forever.

STUDY NOTES

_____

_____

_____

_____

_____

_____

_____

_____

_____

_____

And He said to them all, If any man will come after me, let him deny himself, and take up his cross daily, and follow me.

Luke 9:23

☐ **This Bible fact is something I know by heart.**

☐ **This Bible fact is something I need to study.**

SCRIPTURE NOTES

_____

_____

_____

_____

_____

STUDY SUMMARY

This scripture is essential to have in your arsenal because if you've ever wondered how to deny yourself, the primary answer is to Fast. In a few places within this book I've referenced that me, my wife of 32 years, and our kids have been denying ourselves by Fasting for many years. I've also mentioned that my preference is to live in a continuous Fast, and only eat food only when it is absolutely necessary for me to do so. Fasting for extended periods of time, gives me such an incredible feeling of closeness to God that I honestly want to change my lifestyle to live that way. Use this scripture to teach sacrifice to those who have never done it or want to learn.

STUDY NOTES

_____

_____

_____

_____

_____

_____

_____

_____

_____

_____

And the seventy returned again with joy, saying, Lord, even the devils are subject unto us through thy name. And he said unto them, I beheld Satan as lightning fall from Heaven.

Luke 10:17-18

☐ **This Bible fact is something I know by heart.**

☐ **This Bible fact is something I need to study.**

SCRIPTURE NOTES

_____

_____

_____

_____

_____

STUDY SUMMARY

This scripture is essential to have in your arsenal because when the disciples followed the instructions Jesus gave them, they witnessed exactly what He said would take place. When they came back to give a report, they gave special mention of the fact that demons had to obey what they said do. The response of Jesus was simply that He had witnessed the Devil fall from Heaven like a lightning bolt, when he was evicted and exiled to Earth. This scripture is important for teaching people to believe in boldness and to also proceed in power when they go out to be used as vessels to help heal and set people free.

STUDY NOTES

_____

_____

_____

_____

_____

_____

_____

_____

_____

_____

_____

Behold, I give unto you power to tread on serpents and scorpions, and over all the power of the enemy: and nothing shall by any means hurt you.

Luke 10:19

☐ **This Bible fact is something I know by heart.**

☐ **This Bible fact is something I need to study.**

SCRIPTURE NOTES

_____

_____

_____

_____

_____

_____

STUDY SUMMARY

This scripture is essential to have in your arsenal because not only did Jesus call them to follow Him, so He could teach them how to be fishers of men, He also spent time showing them how they could use His power to heal and deliver others from any strongholds of bondage. Only when the disciples came across a demonic presence that they could not deal with, did Jesus tell them that it was something that could only be dealt with through prayer and Fasting. He gave them further instruction throughout this passage in that He wanted them to know that nothing would be able to harm them along their journey. This scripture is useful for showing people just how powerful the local church on Earth is supposed to be, and can be if we're willing to walk in the same boldness and belief the disciples did.

STUDY NOTES

_____

_____

_____

_____

_____

_____

_____

_____

_____

_____

Jesus answered and said unto him, Verily, verily, I say unto thee, Except a man be born again, he cannot see the kingdom of God.

John 3:3

☐ **This Bible fact is something I know by heart.**

☐ **This Bible fact is something I need to study.**

SCRIPTURE NOTES

_____

_____

_____

_____

_____

STUDY SUMMARY

This scripture is essential to have in your arsenal because in this familiar story, Jesus teaches a man named Nicodemus one very important fact: that being a born-again Christian is vitally important. Being born into the world via the covenant man-woman relationship, or even if its by way of the more modern IVF method, anyone born through these methods experiences a first birth. The second birth happens when a person says *yes* to Jesus being their Lord and Savior and being baptized by water. This process signifies that a person has been born again by entering the water, which essentially says they have been washed by the blood of the lamb for the remission of their sins. This is a vitally important aspect to anyone who is new to church, new to Christ, and new to the custom of becoming a new creature.

STUDY NOTES

_____

_____

_____

_____

_____

_____

_____

_____

_____

For God so loved the world, that he gave His only begotten Son, that whosoever believeth in Him should not perish, but have everlasting life.

John 3:16

☐ **This Bible fact is something I know by heart.**

☐ **This Bible fact is something I need to study.**

SCRIPTURE NOTES

_____

_____

_____

_____

_____

_____

STUDY SUMMARY

This scripture is essential to have in your arsenal because out of all the many dozens of verses and passages contained within this book, this is by far the most important to memorize. In any battles you may face in life, using this as a way to remind yourself and share this truth with others is paramount. This verse is so powerful in the world statistics show that it is the most used, most honored, most recited, and most respected on the planet. The sacrifice of God to give Jesus as a savior for the world, and a redeemer for us to be able to be restored back to God through a relationship with Him, is totally and completely selfless. Jesus had the only pure blood that was capable of being the tool of atonement that would cover the sins of mankind. Teaching why we love God to everyone from childhood through adulthood is the reason we are who we are as Christians and enough can never be said for this act.

STUDY NOTES

_____

_____

_____

_____

_____

_____

_____

_____

_____

_____

Jesus said unto them, If God were your Father, ye would love me: for I proceeded forth and came from God; neither came I of myself, but he sent me. Why do ye not understand my speech? even because ye cannot hear my word. Ye are of your father the devil, and the lusts of your father ye will do. He was a murderer from the beginning, and abode not in the truth, because there is no truth in him. When he speaketh a lie, he speaketh of his own: for he is a liar, and the father of it.

John 8:42-44

☐ **This Bible fact is something I know by heart.**

☐ **This Bible fact is something I need to study.**

SCRIPTURE NOTES

_____

_____

_____

_____

_____

STUDY SUMMARY

This scripture is essential to have in your arsenal because in battle, this is the very scripture you want as the most powerful missile that you can use against Satan. Jesus told this story to a group of people who did not believe. The Devil is the father of lies. For many decades, I've been using this verse as a defense mechanism anytime the adversary tries to plant any crazy thoughts in my mind. It is the one scripture I know that will back him off me each and every single time. While other verses may have to be combined with other scripture to be effective, this one passage that says *the Devil is a liar and there is no truth in him* is still used in most churches by many members.

STUDY NOTES

But ye shall receive power, after that the Holy Ghost is come upon you: and ye shall be witnesses unto me both in Jerusalem, and in all Judaea, and in Samaria, and unto the uttermost part of the Earth.

Acts 1:8

☐ **This Bible fact is something I know by heart.**

☐ **This Bible fact is something I need to study.**

SCRIPTURE NOTES

_____

_____

_____

_____

_____

_____

STUDY SUMMARY

This scripture is essential to have in your arsenal because this is one of the most widely used scriptures for teaching people about the comforter Jesus sent back; the power of the Holy Spirit; the tongues which people speak with when it enters them; and so on. This verse has over the years become more widely known as part of the *Ascension* story. This is an incredible gift to give to people who are unfamiliar with the Holy Spirit and need a basic introduction of what it is and how it works. Even by today's standards we are still infants in the knowledge of all that it can do, but teaching what we do know will help us and others learn about it, and seek after it more and more.

STUDY NOTES

_____

_____

_____

_____

_____

_____

_____

_____

_____

_____

_____

And when the day of Pentecost was fully come, they were all with one accord in one place. And suddenly there came a sound from Heaven as of a rushing mighty wind, and it filled all the house where they were sitting. And there appeared unto them cloven tongues like as of fire, and it sat upon each of them. And they were all filled with the Holy Ghost, and began to speak with other tongues, as the Spirit gave them utterance.

Acts 2:1-4

☐ **This Bible fact is something I know by heart.**

☐ **This Bible fact is something I need to study.**

SCRIPTURE NOTES

_____

_____

_____

_____

_____

_____

STUDY SUMMARY

This scripture is essential to have in your arsenal because the power of the Holy Spirit is how we are able to accomplish the things in our life today that Jesus set examples for us to follow in Biblical times. Without the power of the Holy Spirit, we could not lay hands on people and see them healed; we couldn't command demons to identify themselves and leave someone; we couldn't stand before the masses of people and preach effectively so that it convicts their hearts and they are drawn to Jesus, and so on. Without the power of the Holy Spirit, we could not speak in tongues and communicate with God on a level that those without it cannot achieve. Teach these facts, and continue to learn as much as you can about the Holy Spirit and you will indeed be better of because of it.

STUDY NOTES

_____

_____

_____

_____

_____

_____

_____

_____

_____

And it shall come to pass in the last days, saith God, I will pour out of my Spirit upon all flesh: and your sons and your daughters shall prophesy, and your young men shall see visions, and your old men shall dream dreams:

Acts 2:17

☐ **This Bible fact is something I know by heart.**

☐ **This Bible fact is something I need to study.**

SCRIPTURE NOTES

_____

_____

_____

_____

_____

_____

STUDY SUMMARY

This scripture is essential to have in your arsenal because I'm a living witness of dreaming some very vivid dreams. Some of the dreams are instructional, warning, directional, suggestive, but all are typically very active. I've had visions where I've been sitting or standing next to God, Jesus, the Holy Spirit, Angels, and in such visions I'm either being shown something I need to know; or being given the answer to a question I've asked. Other times I'm shown something about a loved one in my family or a church member or someone who I eventually meet. I believe we are living in the last days. I've seen many signs and evidence. A relationship with God through His Son Jesus the Christ is necessary for us to have any chance of making it to Heaven when we die, or when Jesus comes back to rapture His church.

STUDY NOTES

_____

_____

_____

_____

_____

_____

_____

_____

_____

Therefore let all the house of Israel know assuredly, that God hath made that same Jesus, whom ye have crucified, both Lord and Christ.

Acts 2:36

☐ **This Bible fact is something I know by heart.**

☐ **This Bible fact is something I need to study.**

SCRIPTURE NOTES

_____

_____

_____

_____

_____

_____

STUDY SUMMARY

This scripture is essential to have in your arsenal because even in today's times, there is still much opposition to this verse. The Devil is always busy planting seeds of doubt in people's minds about whether or not Jesus is the Christ, and that He is Lord. As Christians, we know it to be true because the Spirit has confirmed to us that it is. This is why it is so vitally important to continue to teach this to young people and to new believers and to those in unreached and untraveled places in tribes, who have yet to hear about the love of God, and the sacrifice of Jesus, and the free gift of salvation. Even with the Internet, videotaped messages, and audio Podcasts, there are still places on the planet we have yet to reach, thus there is still work to be done.

STUDY NOTES

_____

_____

_____

_____

_____

_____

_____

_____

_____

_____

Now when they heard this, they were pricked in their heart, and said unto Peter and to the rest of the apostles, Men and brethren, what shall we do? Then Peter said unto them, Repent, and be baptized every one of you in the name of Jesus Christ for the remission of sins, and ye shall receive the gift of the Holy Ghost. For the promise is unto you, and to your children, and to all that are afar off, even as many as the Lord our God shall call.

Acts 2:37-39

☐ **This Bible fact is something I know by heart.**

☐ **This Bible fact is something I need to study.**

SCRIPTURE NOTES

_____

_____

_____

_____

_____

_____

STUDY SUMMARY

This scripture is essential to have in your arsenal because in the Pentecostal church Acts 2:38, which reads *then Peter said unto them, Repent, and be baptized every one of you in the name of Jesus Christ for the remission of sins, and ye shall receive the gift of the Holy Ghost* is the scripture that serves as the foundation for their faith. Having been a member of a church congregation based on the Pentecost for five years, I learned and understand the basis for the belief. This is the only scripture that includes Jesus, Baptism, the remission of sins, and the Holy Spirit in the same verse. No other single scripture anywhere in the Bible does this. Even if that does not meet your criteria for a foundation of faith, this verse is useful for many things including teaching these facts both individually and separately.

STUDY NOTES

_____

_____

_____

_____

_____

_____

_____

_____

_____

_____

Neither is there salvation in any other: for there is none other name under Heaven given among men, whereby we must be saved.

Acts 4:12

☐ **This Bible fact is something I know by heart.**

☐ **This Bible fact is something I need to study.**

SCRIPTURE NOTES

_____

_____

_____

_____

_____

_____

STUDY SUMMARY

This scripture is essential to have in your arsenal because as another one of my most favorite memory verses, this is one of the most effective missiles when used against the Devil anytime he attacks you. Satan lost his salvation. His plan is to help you to lose yours too. By simply planting seeds of doubt, and a host of other things in your mind, many people have fallen and according to the Bible, will continue to fall away from the faith. This scripture is useful when teaching people who have questions about other religions and for helping them to understand that following after other gods is not the way to get to Heaven. There is only one way, and that is through Jesus Christ, our Lord and Savior.

STUDY NOTES

_____

_____

_____

_____

_____

_____

_____

_____

_____

_____

_____

There is therefore now no condemnation to them which are in Christ Jesus, who walk not after the flesh, but after the Spirit.

Romans 8:1

☐ **This Bible fact is something I know by heart.**

☐ **This Bible fact is something I need to study.**

SCRIPTURE NOTES

_____

_____

_____

_____

_____

STUDY SUMMARY

This scripture is essential to have in your arsenal because it is yet another of my most favorite verse to commit to memory. When the Devil tries to attack you by reminding you or condemn you or accuse you of something you did wrong in your past, or even in the present, use this scripture to assure him that there is no condemnation for those who are covered by the blood of Christ Jesus. Seeing that he can't be afforded this protection, it typically moves him away from you pretty quickly. In order for us to keep using this invaluable instrument against the enemy, we must continue to walk in the Spirit and not in fulfilling the lusts of our flesh.

STUDY NOTES

_____

_____

_____

_____

_____

_____

_____

_____

_____

_____

_____

What shall we then say to these things? If God be for us, who can be against us?

Romans 8:31

☐ **This Bible fact is something I know by heart.**

☐ **This Bible fact is something I need to study.**

SCRIPTURE NOTES

_____

_____

_____

_____

_____

_____

STUDY SUMMARY

This scripture is essential to have in your arsenal because when I first heard this verse I was a new creature in church. *If God be for us who can be against us* is still one of the most popular and widely used scriptures in sermons today. The truth of the statement speaks loudly to any attack of the adversary, but again, we have some work to do to achieve it. The verse says *if* which means that we have to be certain that God *is* for us. The way we do that is to keep His commandments, and if we haven't, we must confess, repent, ask forgiveness, and keep moving forward being mindful not to commit the sin again. The Bible says that all have sinned and fallen short of the glory of God, so we must do everything we can to be holy and righteous so that this scripture works on our behalf.

STUDY NOTES

_____

_____

_____

_____

_____

_____

_____

_____

_____

_____

That if thou shalt confess with thy mouth the Lord Jesus, and shalt believe in thine heart that God hath raised him from the dead, thou shalt be saved. For with the heart man believeth unto righteousness; and with the mouth confession is made unto salvation.

Romans 10:9-10

☐ **This Bible fact is something I know by heart.**

☐ **This Bible fact is something I need to study.**

SCRIPTURE NOTES

_____

_____

_____

_____

_____

_____

STUDY SUMMARY

This scripture is essential to have in your arsenal because in the Baptist church where I served for 10 years as the right hand to the pastor, this verse *That if thou shalt confess with thy mouth the Lord Jesus, and shalt believe in thine heart that God hath raised him from the dead, thou shalt be saved* serves as the foundation for their faith. This was completely different than the Pentecostal church I served at and attended where Acts 2:38 is the basis for their belief. The scripture in Acts mentions nothing about salvation, as this one in Romans does. However, regardless of who's right, or whether both scriptures were designed to work together and man has interpreted it wrong, both are equally important to the life of every Christian.

STUDY NOTES

_____

_____

_____

_____

_____

_____

_____

_____

_____

_____

And the peace of God, which passeth all understanding, shall keep your hearts and minds through Christ Jesus.

Philippians 4:7

☐ **This Bible fact is something I know by heart.**

☐ **This Bible fact is something I need to study.**

SCRIPTURE NOTES

_____

_____

_____

_____

_____

_____

STUDY SUMMARY

This scripture is essential to have in your arsenal because there are many things on this planet and in this society that can cause us major stress. For example, on the planet, there are all sorts of snakes, serpents, scorpions and spiders, many of which are poisonous. Even though I don't live anywhere near any of them, it still causes me stress just thinking about it, and especially when I visit places where they are native to and known to live. Another example is all the seemingly endless things we think we have to do to keep our house in order, bills paid, spouse happy and content, and kids in line and making progress. This scriptures helps you teach people how to overcome stress before it overshadows and overwhelms them.

STUDY NOTES

_____

_____

_____

_____

_____

_____

_____

_____

_____

_____

I can do all things through Christ which strengtheneth me.

Philippians 4:13

☐ **This Bible fact is something I know by heart.**

☐ **This Bible fact is something I need to study.**

SCRIPTURE NOTES

_____

_____

_____

_____

_____

STUDY SUMMARY

This scripture is essential to have in your arsenal because not only is it one of the most widely used memory verses, I've seen is hanging in many people's bathrooms, kitchens, printed on pictures, vases and other items in their homes. This scripture is the one to use whenever the enemy is attacking any part of your life where he is planting seeds of doubt in your mind about being able to accomplish a certain task such as getting a new job, landing a promotion or raise, starting a new business, launching a new product, or even inventing a new process. There are endless possibilities and pathways that open up when this verse is used with faith behind it, and the Devil doesn't want you to walk down any of them.

STUDY NOTES

_____

_____

_____

_____

_____

_____

_____

_____

_____

_____

_____

Finally, brethren, pray for us, that the word of the Lord may have free course, and be glorified, even as it is with you: And that we may be delivered from unreasonable and wicked men: for all men have not faith. But the Lord is faithful, who shall stablish you, and keep you from evil.

2nd Thessalonians 3:1-3

☐ **This Bible fact is something I know by heart.**

☐ **This Bible fact is something I need to study.**

SCRIPTURE NOTES

_____

_____

_____

_____

_____

STUDY SUMMARY

This scripture is essential to have in your arsenal because this verse contains a request for prayer, a reference to the word, in reverence to giving God glory. It also includes a plea that the reader pray that they will be *delivered from unreasonable and wicked men*. One of the most important parts of Apostle Paul's second letter to the church at Thessalonica is the reminder that *all men do no have faith*. This reminder serves to help us remember that in our Christian walk, there will be times where wicked people will try and treat us with less than right reasons. Their morals may never turn their hearts toward serving God and therefore we must be mindful that *the Lord is faithful and will establish us and keep us from evil*.

STUDY NOTES

_____

_____

_____

_____

_____

_____

_____

_____

_____

_____

For we brought nothing into this world, and it is certain we can carry nothing out. And having food and raiment let us be therewith content. But they that will be rich fall into temptation and a snare, and into many foolish and hurtful lusts, which drown men in destruction and perdition.
For the love of money is the root of all evil: which while some coveted after, they have erred from the faith, and pierced themselves through with many sorrows. But thou, O man of God, flee these things; and follow after righteousness, godliness, faith, love, patience, meekness. Fight the good fight of faith, lay hold on eternal life, whereunto thou art also called, and hast professed a good profession before many witnesses.

1st Timothy 6:7-12

☐ **This Bible fact is something I know by heart.**

☐ **This Bible fact is something I need to study.**

SCRIPTURE NOTES

_____

_____

_____

_____

_____

_____

STUDY SUMMARY

This scripture is essential to have in your arsenal because the wisdom and protection inside this passage points to several things that are used as memory verses. It speaks to contentment, it teaches on the dangers of the love of money, and trains us as people of God to run from these things and pursue that which can inject holiness into our lives. It continues on with a bit of encouragement and more instruction for those who Jesus has brought from their past into their new life in the present. I'm a living witness that God has brought me a mighty long way. I can never thank God enough for His grace and mercy, love and kindness, goodness, patience and understanding, over the entire length of my life. Another book of mine titled *All The Ways* speaks a little to how grateful I am in that it contains dozens of passages of poetry useful for helping to remind us of just how good was, is, and will be to us.

STUDY NOTES

_____

_____

_____

_____

_____

_____

_____

_____

_____

For God hath not given us the spirit of fear; but of power, and of love, and of a sound mind.

2nd Timothy 1:7

☐ **This Bible fact is something I know by heart.**

☐ **This Bible fact is something I need to study.**

SCRIPTURE NOTES

_____

_____

_____

_____

_____

_____

STUDY SUMMARY

This scripture is essential to have in your arsenal because fear is one of the primary weapons the Devil uses against us. This scriptures is useful for standing on the fact that fear is not of God. In most churches you'll hear it described as **F**alse **E**vidence **A**ppearing **R**eal. Within this is how we also recognize that God has given us power over the enemy; He shows us that He loves us unconditionally; and He wants us to keep our focus on Him through Christ, so that our character stays within the framework of a sound mind, loving heart, giving Spirit, full of faith with works that give Him glory. Our lives as Christians are outlined in detail throughout the Bible and this very popular verse is yet another one of those to commit to memory.

STUDY NOTES

_____

_____

_____

_____

_____

_____

_____

_____

_____

_____

And the Lord shall deliver me from every evil work, and will preserve me unto His heavenly kingdom: to whom be glory for ever and ever. Amen.

2nd Timothy 4:18

☐ This Bible fact is something I know by heart.

☐ This Bible fact is something I need to study.

SCRIPTURE NOTES

_____

_____

_____

_____

_____

STUDY SUMMARY

This scripture is essential to have in your arsenal because Ephesians chapter six teaches us that *we wrestle not against flesh and blood, but against principalities, against powers, against the rulers of the darkness of this world, against spiritual wickedness in high places.* In this scripture God teaches us that He shall deliver us from every evil thing including demons, darkness, and the Devil, that works against us. These are things that we often cannot see, and don't recognize until they are upon us. God delivering us from it is a dynamic way to teach others how they can get through it also.

STUDY NOTES

_____

_____

_____

_____

_____

_____

_____

_____

_____

_____

_____

_____

If any of you lack wisdom, let him ask of God, that giveth to all men liberally, and upbraideth not; and it shall be given him.

James 1:5

☐ **This Bible fact is something I know by heart.**

☐ **This Bible fact is something I need to study.**

SCRIPTURE NOTES

_____

_____

_____

_____

_____

STUDY SUMMARY

This scripture is essential to have in your arsenal because if you ever had the opportunity to ask a question of any General that has ever served in God's Army, or in the United States Armed Services, they will probably all tell you that without wisdom they would not be effective in battle. The same is true for you. When you are doing battle against the enemy, whether it is for you or with you standing in the gap for someone else, you must have wisdom that will lend itself to strategy in order to be successful on the battlefield. We don't enter into war not expecting to win. We expect to defeat the enemy. This scripture teaches us that when we need wisdom God will grant it to us proportionally. Once we have it we can continue to represent Him dutifully.

STUDY NOTES

_____

_____

_____

_____

_____

_____

_____

_____

_____

Submit yourselves therefore to God. Resist the Devil, and he will flee from you.

James 4:7

☐ **This Bible fact is something I know by heart.**

☐ **This Bible fact is something I need to study.**

SCRIPTURE NOTES

_____

_____

_____

_____

_____

_____

STUDY SUMMARY

This scripture is essential to have in your arsenal because until and unless we learn to resist the Devil, he will keep bothering us. This verse is an incredible way to remind ourselves that all we have to do is submit to God and use His word to resist the Devil and Satan will indeed run from us. To Satan, God's word is like an armor-piercing bullet. It cuts him deeply. It is truth that he cannot stand to hear. It is his nemesis. There are many ways written throughout this book that teach us, train us, show us, and give example of how to use these scriptures, verses and passages to resist the Devil, and it is now your responsibility to use this knowledge yourself, and to also pass it along to anyone else that you know does not have it in their arsenal.

STUDY NOTES

_____

_____

_____

_____

_____

_____

_____

_____

_____

And the Devil that deceived them was cast into the lake of fire and brimstone, where the beast and the false prophet are, and shall be tormented day and night for ever and ever.

Revelation 20:10

☐ **This Bible fact is something I know by heart.**

☐ **This Bible fact is something I need to study.**

SCRIPTURE NOTES

_____

_____

_____

_____

_____

STUDY SUMMARY

This scripture is essential to have in your arsenal because deception is the Devil's design. He wants us to look at it long enough to do what Eve did in the Garden of Eden and stare of focus on it so that it begins to distort our God-given ability to discern the evil of it from the goodness of God. This scripture is very close to the last ones in the Bible, but the one that is quite possibly the most important in all of the Bible as it relates to answering the age old question of *Lord when will all this destruction and desolation and demonization end?* As a Christian, you should know the answer to this question or at least be able to teach it to others from Matthew chapter 24 and the book of Revelation. Use this and all the scriptures contained in this Bible study book as tools and ammunition for your arsenal. Commit as much as you can to memory, study the rest, but always be ready to recite them when you need them the most.

STUDY NOTES

_____

_____

_____

_____

_____

_____

_____

_____

_____

END OF BOOK
READING SUGGESTIONS

+ The Gospel of Jesus Christ
(which is comprised of Matthew, Mark, Luke and John)

+ The Acts of the Apostles
Acts 1:1 to 28:31
One chapter per day should take less than one month.

+ The Epistles of Apostle Paul
(which is comprised of Romans through Philemon)

+ The Book of Hebrews

+ The Epistles of James, Peter, John and Jude

+ The Book of Revelation
Revelation 1:1 to 22:21
One chapter per day should take less than one month.

Battle
BONUS

Four of my most favorite scriptures, verses and passages and a challenge to you to write your own Study Summary!

Battle Bonus

The Lord said unto my Lord, Sit thou at my right hand, until I make thine enemies thy footstool.

Psalm 110:1
[Enemies Footstool]

☐ **This Bible fact is something I know by heart.**

☐ **This Bible fact is something I need to study.**

SCRIPTURE NOTES

_____

_____

_____

_____

_____

_____

YOUR OWN STUDY SUMMARY

_____

_____

_____

_____

_____

_____

_____

_____

_____

STUDY NOTES

_____

_____

_____

_____

_____

_____

_____

_____

_____

Battle Bonus

And he gave some, *apostles*; and some, *prophets*; and some, *evangelists*; and some, *pastors* and *teachers*; For the perfecting of the saints, for the work of the ministry, for the edifying of the body of Christ: Till we all come in the unity of the faith, and of the knowledge of the Son of God, unto a perfect man, unto the measure of the stature of the fullness of Christ:

Ephesians 4:11-13
[Five Fold Ministry]

☐ This Bible fact is something I know by heart.

☐ This Bible fact is something I need to study.

SCRIPTURE NOTES

_____

_____

_____

_____

_____

YOUR OWN STUDY SUMMARY

_____

_____

_____

_____

_____

_____

_____

_____

_____

STUDY NOTES

_____

_____

_____

_____

_____

_____

_____

_____

_____

_____

Battle Bonus

Finally, my brethren, be strong in the Lord, and in the power of his might. Put on the whole armour of God, that ye may be able to stand against the wiles of the devil. For we wrestle not against flesh and blood, but against principalities, against powers, against the rulers of the darkness of this world, against spiritual wickedness in high places. Wherefore take unto you the whole armour of God, that ye may be able to withstand in the evil day, and having done all, to stand. Stand therefore, having your loins girt about with truth, and having on the breastplate of righteousness; And your feet shod with the preparation of the gospel of peace; Above all, taking the shield of faith, wherewith ye shall be able to quench all the fiery darts of the wicked. And take the helmet of salvation, and the sword of the Spirit, which is the word of God: Praying always with all prayer and supplication in the Spirit, and watching thereunto with all perseverance and supplication for all saints;

Ephesians 6:10-18
[God's Armor]

☐ **This Bible fact is something I know by heart.**

☐ **This Bible fact is something I need to study.**

SCRIPTURE NOTES

_____

_____

_____

_____

_____

YOUR OWN STUDY SUMMARY

_____

_____

_____

_____

_____

_____

_____

_____

_____

STUDY NOTES

_____

_____

_____

_____

_____

_____

_____

_____

_____

_____

Battle Bonus

But the fruit of the Spirit is love, joy, peace, longsuffering, gentleness, goodness, faith, meekness, temperance: against such there is no law.

Galatians 5:22-23
[Fruit of the Spirit]

☐ This Bible fact is something I know by heart.

☐ This Bible fact is something I need to study.

SCRIPTURE NOTES

_____

_____

_____

_____

_____

YOUR OWN STUDY SUMMARY

STUDY NOTES

+ **Books**
+ **Videos**
+ **Classes**
+ **Podcasts**
+ **Interviews**
and much more at
PastorKeith.org

The
EPILOGUE

CLOSING THOUGHTS

Study methods are critical to learning how to memorize scripture. Why do you need to memorize scripture? Simple. Wherever you are, at any time of the day, in any situation, whether you're sitting in a meeting or doing ministry, the Devil can suddenly attack you with something out of left field.

It can be a thought that he plants in your mind, or he can use someone else to start an argument with you, which is why you need to always be mindful, be prepared, and be ready to respond, just as Jesus did when the Devil was allowed to tempt Him during His Fast of 40 days and 40 nights.

You likely won't recognize the attack because of the slick way Satan does things. He twists people's words, in fact, he even twists God's word. So the attack can be as subtle as something you never imagined could surface.

I recommend several study methods throughout this book but one of the most effective that I typically recommend is using the memory of you mind to help you memorize scripture to use against Satan. Your mind is capable of computing, categorizing, and collecting data at such a broad volume that you will never run out of space to carry or contain it all.

Let your memory be the tool you use to help you memorize scripture. You will be glad you did. Especially when an attack comes and you immediately respond without thinking about it. When it comes natural to you to fight fear with faith, and when you've reached a level of defense where you are in control of your offense, you've already beat the enemy at his own game.

Pastor Keith

www.ingramcontent.com/pod-product-compliance
Lightning Source LLC
Chambersburg PA
CBHW022117080426
42734CB00006B/160